Another Desert:
Jewish Poetry of New Mexico

ANOTHER
DESERT

JEWISH POETRY
OF NEW MEXICO

Edited by

JOAN LOGGHE & MIRIAM SAGAN

Poetic License
This is a work of imagination. Any use of similes or metaphors relating
to actual people living or dead is art. It contains truths not supported
by facts.

Acknowledgments and permissions appear in the contributors section.

Cover Design: Janice St. Marie
Book Design: Judith Rafaela
Cover Art: Diana Bryer "Backroom Ritual" and "Rabbi Lynn"
Printed in the United States of America

FIRST EDITION
ISBN 0-9644196-9-6

Library of Congress Cataloging-in-Publication Data

Another desert : Jewish poetry of New Mexico / edited by Joan
    Logghe & Miriam Sagan. --1st edition
        p. cm.
    Includes bibliographical references and index.
    ISBN 0-96441960906 (alk. paper)
    1. American Poetry--New Mexico. 2. Jewish religious poetry,
    American--New Mexico. 3. American poetry--Jewish authors.
    4. Jews--New Mexico--Poetry. I. Logghe, Joan, 1947– .
    II. Sagan, Miriam, 1954– .
    PS571.N6A56   1998
    811' .540808924'09789--dc21   98-34804
                                                             CIP

Sherman Asher Publishing
PO Box 2853
Santa Fe, NM 87504
Changing the World One Book at a Time™

To our parents

Harry Slesinger of blessed memory
Beti Slesinger Schwartz

Eli Jacob Sagan
Frimi Giller Sagan

CONTENTS

CONVERSOS

FOREWORD

The history of Jewish settlement in New Mexico is often portrayed in terms of descendants of Spanish and Portuguese crypto-Jews fleeing persecution of the Holy Office of the Inquisition at the end of the 1500s — or of German merchants trekking across the Santa Fe Trail in the mid-nineteenth century, establishing themselves in the commercial centers of Santa Fe, Taos, and Las Vegas.

Indeed, these themes comprise an integral part of our Jewish heritage. But the story is far more complex than this. History also encompasses more recent arrivals — from Russia and Eastern Europe around the turn of the twentieth century, refugees from Nazi persecution in the 1930s and 40s, and more recently, American Jews escaping urban problems of the East and West coasts and Midwest, in search of "The Good Life" here in the Southwest.

What all these immigrants have in common is that they all were searching for something that they felt they lacked — freedom, security, peace of mind. But despite the magnificence of the New Mexico landscape, the warmth of the people, and the very special quality of the *ambiente*, for many immigrants the search continues.

The works contained in this volume reflect this search. Some seek answers retrospectively and introspectively in old lands and cultures. Others probe Hispanic and Native American values for the solution to their anxieties. Several of the poems reflect the theme of pain of past experiences — some from the Inquisition, others from the Holocaust, and still others from cultural marginality.

The compilation in one volume of so many moving and profound expressions of the Jewish experience in New Mexico, represents a unique window through which future generations will gain valuable insights with respect to our culture in the closing years of the twentieth century.

Stan M. Hordes, Ph.D.
Adjunct Research Professor
Latin American Institute
University of New Mexico

INTRODUCTION

The first Jews to come to New Mexico arrived at the end of the sixteenth century. These were the Spanish conversos, Sephardic Jews who had converted to Catholicism in 1492 but who were still persecuted by the Inquisition. In 1598, several of them trekked north from Mexico City with Juan de Oñate, one step ahead of prison and torture. The Inquisition never came to the territory that would be New Mexico, and the settlers set up their lives in small villages, following a Catholic way of life and yet some still retaining Jewish customs and identity. It is a testimony to the strength of this identity that four hundred years later our anthology contains the work of such poets as Isabelle Medina Sandoval, descended from the original Spanish settlers who accompanied Oñate to New Mexico.

The nineteenth century brought the opening of the Santa Fe Trail and with it a wave of Northern European Jewish immigrants. While observant Jews tended to stay on the east coast, building a communal life, the more adventurous pioneers followed the Santa Fe Trail from Independence, Missouri to New Mexico—territory conquered by the United States in 1846. German Jewish peddlers arrived and built emporiums for trade in Las Vegas and the towns along the Rio Grande. One of these immigrants, Julia Staab, is described in Jean Nordhaus's poem "Santa Fe: A Jewish Wife."

It wasn't until the 1880s that the Eastern Europeans came west—Jews fleeing pogroms and crowding New York's lower east side. Again, it was the adventurers who came west to remote New Mexico. And New Mexico seemed equally remote to the Jewish scientists and their families who arrived on the Hill in Los Alamos during the building of the atomic bomb, whether they were urbanites like Robert Oppenheimer, or refugees from Hitler.

The majority of contributors to this book can only be described as the most recent wave of Jewish immigration to New Mexico. Quintessential baby boomers—hippies whose cars broke down on the way to Haight-Ashbury or spiritual seekers in wide open spaces who settled down, joined the professions, raised families—we are here today. There are the pioneers such as Bill Gersh and Max Finstein, more members of the Beat

Generation who settled in a then isolated Taos. But whether it is Judyth Hill, raised in Manhattan and living in the wide country near Mora, or Phyllis Hotch, far from her early years in the Bronx among Jewish and Italian neighbors, the Jewish writers of New Mexico now call this landscape home.

The anthology grew naturally out of the community of Jewish poets in New Mexico. Temple Beth Shalom in Santa Fe began hosting poetry readings in its main sanctuary in the early 1990s. Poets such as Judyth Hill, Miriam Sagan, Joan Logghe, Judith Rafaela, and Barbara Rockman would read to overflow crowds. The Temple also published one of its annual calendars adorned by the work of local artists and writers, including Josh Rappaport's "Shavuos" poem. The New Mexico Jewish Historical Society also incorporated literary programs into its annual conferences, whether poetry readings, an award to Henry Roth of Albuquerque shortly before his death, or a presentation on the Taos poets. Conferences also showcased visual artists from Anita Rodriguez to Diana Bryer who dealt with Jewish and crypto-Jewish themes, in turn inspiring writers. Rabbi Lynn Gottlieb's congregation Nahalat Shalom in Albuquerque also provided a flowering of the visual and literary arts. All of this activity highlighted an informal community of poets who were drawing on many of the same themes and resources. This book brings them together.

As editors, we divided the anthology into sections that held thematic material. For New Mexico Jewish writers, certain themes recur almost obsessively. First there is the image of Diaspora, or of a scattered people. For the writers here, this seems to pertain as much to our own leaving of roots behind as to the exile of the Jewish people. America is a widescape, almost too big to contain. Natalie Goldberg confesses "I Tried to Marry America" while Jenny Goldberg mourns the loss of a specific home to the Lama Mountain forest fire. And there is the land—a high desert of Exodus, the wilderness where the Jews wandered after Egypt. Wanderers all, these poets embrace the contradictions of travel and home.

The cycle of the Jewish year is also saturated by the New Mexico experience. Tashlich is performed in a precious desert river, Passover coincides with the sight of Good Friday pilgrims making a holy journey to the

Santuario de Chimayó. Yehudis Fishman in her "Shabbos in Santa Fe" can't help but notice where she is—this is a very particular Shabbos in time and place.

If the holidays create a sacred cycle of time, personal time is more linear. The section on ancestors, family, and psychic inheritance points to where we came from, often the Russia and Poland of our grandparents, as in "My Odessa" by Ánnah Sobelman. Then there is the larger inheritance, of story, commentary, midrash, retelling, such as Carol Moldaw's reweaving of a Hasidic tale in "Reb Shmerl" or Judyth Hill's new look at "Mrs. Noah."

Memory is an antidote to loss, whether individual or collective. There is Joan Logghe's tiny but poignant elegy for Bill Gersh, "One Wild Jew Missing" while other poems mourn lost family members and the Holocaust. Allen Ginsberg was the first American Jewish poet to grab Kaddish and turn it into a Walt Whitmanesque lament that burst boundaries. These poems all say Kaddish in their own way.

The history of the Sephardic Jews in New Mexico captures the imagination of many of the poets here. It is a compelling theme of displacement and survival that seizes writers from Robin Becker in "The Crypto Jews" to Consuelo Luz in her lyrics "One Fine Day Full of Love." Elmo Mondragón speaks from ancestral experience in "After the Inquisition." Perhaps the Jewish poets of New Mexico are unique in that for us the events of 1492 are as vivid as those of the Holocaust.

At root, however, these are ultimately poems of faith—in the beauty of the desert, in the survival of tradition and memory, and ultimately in the ability of language to contain and express experience. The desert of New Mexico has been good to its poets, giving us inspiration and community.

Miriam Sagan
Santa Fe, NM
1998

EDITOR'S NOTE

This is the book I can take home to dinner. I was raised as a reform Jew, living on the same block as Rodef Shalom Temple in Pittsburgh, a temple so reform that in my day they didn't do Bar Mitzvahs. I loved Hebrew, the stories, and especially ethics. I belonged to the Jewish Youth group and was confirmed there. As a college student and young adult, my Jewish identity was confined mainly to Lox and Bagels, the foods of our famous family brunches. I thought brunch was a Jewish holiday.

Since I married a man raised as a Catholic farm boy, my Jewish identity has been through several stages. When I had my own family, after moving to New Mexico, Sabbath became part of the fabric. The week felt better if I made a Sabbath dinner: candles, wine, bread, and prayer. I began celebrating Passover with poet Judyth Hill who was studying Judaism intensively. Then Passover moved to my house where I have over twenty people each year. I remember the Rosh Hashanah I couldn't get to temple because my arroyo was running so high from a flash flood. I made stuffed cabbage to observe.

Rabbis Lynn Gottlieb of Albuquerque, Nahum Ward-Lev of Santa Fe, and Carol Carp of Taos informed my adult understanding of this traditionally patriarchal religion. I found this year, while attending High Holiday services in three congregations, that I felt welcome and comfortable in all three communities.

The idea for this book came to me at night. Part of it came from Poet's Mind. I knew that many of my Jewish friends were writing wonderful pieces based on their studies of Judaism set against life in New Mexico. Part of the idea came from Soul Mind. I wanted to do something from and for my roots, my Old Country of Pittsburgh via two immigrant families, one from Lithuania and one from Hungary. Part of the idea came from Retail Mind. My family were business people. I saw the enthusiasm and interest in Diana Bryer's crypto-Jewish images, and felt a book graced by her cover art would have a strong appeal.

16

When Miriam Sagan and I sat on my bed New Year's morning of 1997, warm drinks in hand after a sleepover, I mentioned my idea. She said "Jewish Anthology!" She asked if I wanted a collaborator. I loved the idea of working with her and the chance to spend legitimate time together. We were on. I have found her to be a joy to work with besides being the fastest reader in the West.

A note on style and language. In keeping with the spirit of pluralism so prevalent here in the West we have preserved the variants of spellings for the Ladino, Yiddish, and Hebrew words.

It's amazing to feel in hand what I saw in mind years ago. I hope for you too, that it will be a book to take home to dinner, to read from at holidays, and to inspire you in your particular way of being Jewish.

Joan Logghe
La Puebla, NM
1998

DIASPORA

Are we commanded by God to wander?
or driven by a restlessness of spirit?
Abraham and Sarah sent out by God's command.
Did their friends feast them before leaving,
and with subtle hostility enumerate the perils?
I can see them in the desert
"Travel light"

—Judith Rafaela
from LECH LECHA

Natalie Goldberg

I TRIED TO MARRY AMERICA

I tried hard to marry America
To let its rivers swim in me
and the lost small farm graveyards
be the death of my people too

I tried to marry America
the red freckled hand of a man I loved
carried a lit tree into my home in December
I ate scallop stew the body of Christ in the evening

I tried hard to marry the Ohio Valley
and Sandusky County
I tried to bring Cleveland to sit at my table and
eat gefilte fish
to hide the afikomen in Arkansas
and help San Francisco when her kippah fell off
I tried to call in the Shabbos bride over the plains of Nebraska
and break braided egg bread over the Dakotas
To make God of the Universe the majesty of the Adirondacks

I tried to make a wedding band of wheat
and wear the veil of lilacs leaning over a picket white fence
I tried to get the accent off my lips
and wipe the honey from my face

LEAVING ISRAEL: A LAMENT
for Carol Soutor

I'm sorry for the empty afternoons when I wanted to go home
    and for the letters I wrote when I could have
    been walking up Zion, down the Kidron Valley
I have had too many cold nights and wind blown days

I'm sorry Batia and I couldn't have seen each other more
    and I have grown old from being young in these last months
I'll miss the tea in glasses, Tel Aviv far away
    and the lights of too many cities in long distances through
    the night
I'll miss the pale light on the Temple Mount, the mad donkeys,
    bare hills near Jericho and the abandoned dirt Arab homes

Forgive me, Jerusalem, if I did not love you enough, rode your
    busses down the spine of whistling memory, your stones,
    broken cemetery on Mount Olives, did not wait centuries with
    you for the pale donkey carrying the Messiah into your
    golden gates
Forgive me for still loving my ex-husband though he is not Jewish
    and the nights I still want him deep in my skin and the
    minutes that have passed blooming irises
The old man begging at the bottom of the underpass at the Central
    Bus Station who I never gave coins to—forgive me, and the
    half light down Strauss after the Turkish baths with the quick
    long coated Hassids, moving in the dying day like an old song
    down the hill
Forgive me for being modern and still wanting religion and being
    scared alone in the Old City
And forgive my dreams at night that sleep with too many men
    and sit with women for hours in coffee shops in lost streets
    at the edge of town
And forgive me for loving the desert, way beyond sound or thought
    my eyes opening or sense, and being too old to move anywhere
    anymore

Miriam Sagan

THE GOD OF THE JEWS

Before I let fly my wrist daggers
And became an importer of coffee and brass
Before I kept green macaws
And listened to the cawing of crows
Before I scattered
I prayed to a wall facing east.

Oh Jerusalem,
Most female of cities,
Where moonlight
Is a staircase leading down
And where even a housepainter's ladder
Leaning against an adobe wall
Might encourage angels
To a dreaming Jacob.

Like Jacob I could put my head against a stone
Or make a pillow from the skull of a cow,
Like Israel I went out walking
And crossed a wasteland of ant hills, scrub, and cactus thorn;
There on the high tabletop the mesa
With a sacred mountain to the north
And a pyramid built by a mad architect
On a scaffolding of beer cans, tires and mud—
And although I walked, as if on ocean
Behind me still the pyramid,
Until I turned, returning toward it
A Giza out of bondage.

Somewhere maybe there is a God of the Jews
A God who scents a meaning out of history
A God I will never meet
Not a burning bush, or shining tree.
And although we kept our china packed in suitcases
Although we caught or missed the last train out,
And stood on a platfrom in a great expanse
Of snow and tundra, our breath
Hanging before us like a pillar of smoke,
And although the sun scorched us by day
And the moon shivered all night—
Despite the fact our last names meant we fled,
And in the end, on islands, we were refugees
Still we did not go crying out to God
But made a sustenance of bread; of wine—a word.

WAILING WALL

Why, somewhere between sleep and waking
I saw myself at the wall in Jerusalem
Twenty years ago—too young and stupid
To pray, or stuff a crumpled desire
Penciled on paper into a crevice
Ululations of dark women throwing hard candy
At a bar-mitzvah. I was a stranger.
Where did I come from?
Bad tribesmen without horses,
Who cut off their foreskins
Poured blood on a stone;
Silent women with jars on their heads
Who sat at the gate
To judge and prophesy.
The jews before they knew
They were Jews
Before God spoke
When they raided cattle
Someplace unchanging and olive-colored
With far-off mountains.
The Arch of Titus
With its soldiers and captured menorah
Says we passed into history
And then passed out of it completely again.
Now I am sure there is a sweeper
Besides the desert wind
To clear those prayers each night
Scattered beneath the luminous Dome of the Rock
And the silver mosque
More beautiful than a woman's throat
Under the Moslem moon
And a zodiac of golden fish.

Who sweeps?
An old bent man with a broom
In a frayed black coat
He is a Charlie Chaplin
A butcher from Brooklyn
An Auschwitz survivor
A seller of falafel
He is alone but his eyes don't blink back tears
As he pushes away the prayers
Of the childless, the sick, the dispossessed
That cover the wall
With reproach, like a child's cry, a dove of hope.

Gene Frumkin

EXPECTING ME

I would greet myself zealously,
suspecting I might forget to arrive
                    and lie in the water,
                              dreaming.
                    Mother and father,
                              buried
          in Congregation Beth Israel's cemetery,
would they know me
                    now that I have grown older
          and find less humor in nature?

          The feast is held on Sunday
after an ordinary Sabbath.
I keep expecting myself—the food smells
                              like angels.
                    I have noticed
                    great crowds swarming
                through the sunlight.
Experimentally, I touch where my heart
                    should be.
          I am deserted inside myself.
          I realize that life is exaggerated.

Will I come alone or with others?
          My parents, I know, expect me
as if I were Elijah
                    come to collect his respect
                    from the Passover dinner.
          I have never seen him
          even though my father
hid the matzoh under his pillowed seat
                              every time.

I will come, having lived with
                the worms.   My eyes
                will be powdered with dust.
        Still, I will know my name
and welcome the presence that lives
                        on Earth
                whatever his faith might lack.
        I will grow
into myself like a flower from its precept.
The best news reveals itself in cycles
                of come and go.
                I have wandered far
into the thick horizon where no Hebrews live.
I am ready to return to myself,
the one who expects Lazarus in the mail.

Gene Frumkin

THE SINGER OF MANOA STREET

Reading Isaac Singer, I spring back
into my Jewish body. I take notes
on my left palm in a strange script,
although I recognize the word "onions"
and also "strategic demons." From somewhere
a gust of wind passes through me;
it smells like exalted soup. Shall I sew
a yellow Star of David onto each of my
aloha shirts?
          Clearly, I must stop
reading Singer. One short work of his
seems enough to bring God's absence
into my room. Soon, while I am alone,
someone will look into my mirror who isn't me.
I remember my father, my mother,
my wife, all well-rested in the soil
of our American republic. These memories
are scarcely ideas.
             It is too late
to put the book down. I'll go on
in my short pants, the nice fat boy still,
walking the streets of Honolulu,
observing how little remains
of my past. Each year there is less,
each year a fresh body of knowledge
moves through my blood and says,
"I'm home now. Just let me sleep."

Of course Singer is not to blame,
his job is telling stories. If I feel
more Jewish, it is personal, not too serious:
what I feel these days is like
last night's half moon. But I still won't sign
the Covenant, which chose me so eugenically—
"You're a Jew, kid. Don't chase after shiksas."
I'll think more about Jehovah, Who knows everything,
and also about how sly and careless nature is.

Max Finstein

EASTER PEACE

It is my day: a jew crucified they say
but in this county none knows I am
alive. sat peacefully

all day here in Arroyo Seco.
sipped bourbon
one dexamil a little hashish.
watched birds.

Bird. the children left me alone
I read poems I did my taxes
wrote one poem.

Max Finstein

FOR THE CHAMBER OF COMMERCE

I could be the first jewish governor of New Mexico.
With you behind me we'd have water
here in this north water
and plenty of it. With you
behind me i'd be the first jewish
governor of the pueblo
here in this land of enchantment
and winter recreation
would boom with the largest
ski lift erected this year
i'd be the first jewish
indian to slalom down
wheeler
and paint it as I go down
with not too hot
enchiladas
on velvet. Coronado's helmet
as escutcheon for the Democrats.

Judith Rafaela

WANDERING JEW

As I journey through times and places
strange and enticing
I shrug my Judaism on and off like an old shawl.
Sometimes worn for fashion
to promenade at holidays
or when the nights are cold and lonely.
The family says,
"that old thing, again?"
To wear it calls attention to our difference.
How easily, then, we slip from routine
from the flow of our lives measured
in candles and blessing
to the seduction of the
multiple personality gods.
Not that ours,
with the 13 names,
keeps boundaries like we've been told.

Drawn to the smell of incense
the chanting and gongs.
Dance with the goddess in the full moon.
The promise of Joy without the restrictions.
I wrap the shawl tighter against the chill of aging
until it chokes me.
The great weight of history bows my back.
I throw it off, go weeks pretending I don't notice
I'm eating shellfish.
Pack it away in sterile hotel rooms
where I light no fires of faith.
But, oh, when community gathers
I have a soft silken shawl.
Golden threads of pride and tradition
caressing my back and breasts
with the movements of the song.
Sacred for prayer.

KITCHEN TABLE

Sometimes I see the kitchen table
As clouds and rain and trees,
Sometimes as the labor of the carpenter
The truck driver, the maker of the lathe.

Sometimes I don't see any of its divinity,
And treat it merely as a thing
That needs wiping.

Sometimes I see the kitchen table
As floating in space,
And me, tentatively placed
Feebly saying grace.

Shuli Lamden

AN ARK OF WOOD

Make thee an ark of wood, God says to Moses.
My father built the ark for our synagogue—
such rich wood, dark red. Dad assembled the ark

on our playroom floor, then lined it with deep green carpet.
A box, a new toy, smelling of sawdust.
My brothers and I climbed in and out.

I could crawl in, slide shut the doors,
live in the ark. I could live like the law,
with the law.

It is not too hard for thee, neither is it far off…
The word is very nigh unto thee, in thy mouth
and in thy heart, that thou mayest do it.

But I haven't done it. I've become accustomed
to being the only Jew in a room, to explaining
my Hebrew name over and over, the way

my mother's father Louis, in his small Midwestern town,
drove from church to church on a speaking tour, to explain
his life as a Lithuanian Jew.

One minister, fearing that Louis would be lost
(to the Presbyterians instead of the Methodists), once asked,
"Louis, if you weren't Jewish, what would you be?"

My grandfather answered, "I'd be ashamed of myself."
Sometimes I am ashamed of myself.
Sometimes I do not know who I am.

When I was little, I asked my mother
about the other people: "If they're not Jewish,
who are they?" I don't remember her answer.

Yehudis Fishman

SHIFTING BONES

1

Moshe the Levite, fled
the luxuriance of Egypt
to the barrens of Midyan,
a prince in exile
rescued by Yitro, priest of many idols.
Levi Spiegelberg, bold entrepreneur,
fled from the old world of oppression
into the flatlands of New Mexico.
Abandoned by his family, his rotting bones
were rescued by Archbishop Lamy.

2

The generation of the desert
plodded through corregated sand,
each family leading ninety donkeys
laden with garments, gold and silver—
taking a long route to avoid
strewn bones from the tribe of Ephraim,
who left Egypt 30 years too soon
and were massacred by Philistines,
the tribe of dry bones in the vision of Ezekiel—
whose flight to freedom could not forever be denied,
but would spring up fresh in a future film.

3

Generations of white men pushing west,
longing for empty spaces,
for trees whose arms shot upward,
whose arms provided wood for hatchets
and rifles for riddling red men's teepees.

They did not even sigh at the bleached bones of people
who were one with the land and the buffalo,
who treasured water more than glossy gadgets,
people who waited for the fairness of a new dawn
to redress their blood.

4
I am a wandering Jew
who ran from the tin-can cities of the east,
meandering through the winding alleys,
up and down the silent scorched slopes of Santa Fe,
hoping for freedom,
and groping for treasures,
seeking the elusive Luz—
the bone that defies the ruse of disintegration.

5
I see a roadrunner
darting across the mesa
while a dove trembles
in the cleft of a striped rock.
Nations of the world will bear gifts
to the regal redeemer, Moshiach:
Jewish souls hiding
among the thorn bushes.

Jenny Goldberg

SONG OF WILDFIRE

Many waters cannot quench love,
neither can the floods drown it:
if a man would give all the
substance of his house for love,
it would utterly be contemned.
—*Song of Solomon*

Out of the wilderness rose pillars of smoke,
wild flames on the ridge. I ran to grab you

from bed. We met in a cleft of rock above treeline,
recognized some shadow on the iris, the lost shoe

in the desert and took love for a noun,
fire in the chamber, tinge of jasmine, blood

of peacevine cherry tomatoes on your dress.
We thought love was a hanging begonia that bloomed

pink flowers all year, a menorah on the mantel,
cornflower teapot on the table and when

the teapot cracked, the hanging pot shattered,
menorah gone to ash, the gift had been rescinded.

You blamed God: our home on the mountain burned,
our neighbor's untouched.

I said, *Wildfire's not the Angel of Death. Chosen,*
not burned. Our bed is green.

Days after the fire, love became a verb, passive,
something done to us or not done. Trees killed

or passed over. On the dirt road, people stood by easels,
painted ruins, charcoaled and oiled us, snap-shot

37

and framed us. Some shook their heads, squinted eyes
as if those motions of disbelief might detach them

from the losses they imagined. You no longer
etched me, saw me, touched me, but fingered

the mad face on the hearth—holes charred in plaster,
the monster hunks of melted refrigerator and sink.

My fingers combed ashes for love shards, found
the menorah burned to a nine-pointed star.

You threw it in the ditch, which had dried.
Love the noun left us loveless.

You packed your backpack, filled the baskets
on your bike, put on your white desert hat and rode

into the garden of burnt fruit. I watched you
bump past the black apple. As you rode through the tunnel

of half-blackened pines, love became an active verb.
I loved the diminishing white point of your hat

disappearing in the forest, the vanilla scent of burnt bark.
That night I slept by the roofless adobe south wall.

Hate burned to ash with the rest of our treasures.
I loved the memory of you tugging on the frying pan

welded to the stove, the hollow drops of rain,
loved the feel of everything gone,

night without lights, food without plates,
love without a roof to hold it in.

FORGOTTEN ONES

God of Abraham
God of Isaac Jacob
God of Rebecca Sarah Ruth
of Lillian Rosensweig and Aunt Priscilla
with her yellow marigolds in Brooklyn
and the newstand by the subway entrance
God of Esther planting willows in Long Island
and pink hibiscus in Miami
God of mother Sylvie Ann with her story lid eyes
and the mouth of wonder and her soft miraculous knees
in a cotton nightgown
God of Uncle Manny whitening into old age on his mother's chair

God of the rootless New Yorkers that left New York
God of the rootless Jews who stayed in New York
God of the burning of Poland and the empty Jewish Cemetery
in Warsaw
and Elaine's Aunt in Queens with the numbers on her left arm
and the *Jerusalem Post* and the candies on the coffee table
God of the lost American Jews who have no god
who stand in the streets of Chicago against a blistering winter
that makes the mouth forget cousin Abraham and cousin Isaac
and the forgotten ones in the army
and the forgotten ones in college
and the forgotten ones in Newark New Jersey
after the rich moved out to the suburbs

God of lamplight and candlelight
God of roast chicken and freeze-dried coffee
of old rooms in Miami hotels
full of cockroaches and old people in white sheets
God of skylines along the Florida coast
and pale pink and yellow Palm Beach homes

God of murder and suicide
of Gary's grandfather Mr. Stein
whose name in red cursive neon appeared
near my home on Long Island
selling more chrome for your cars
who jumped from his balcony in Pompano Beach at 83
God of his folded body in the hard sand and stopped heart

God of David Solomon Miriam and Rebecca
Mother of earth and small lean yellow salamanders
green covered rocks by the slapping ocean
and swollen feet in the heat of humid summer
God of cars and wheels
of high rises moving out of the earth into the white sky
and the pink sky at dusk
and the grey sky at dawn

And Mother of stars and noon and gull wings
great bands of turkey buzzards in the south
and tennis in the rain
the wet ball like an old dog's yellow face and the puddles
and green trees
And the soft moment we are alive
at the change of the traffic light
and God and Mother of weeping death
tears in eyelashes
Bless Us   Bless Us   Bless Us
through all the rivers of time

WEAPON

time to build a survival weapon
one that's silent and powerful
one that can be used in Kansas
and the Dakotas, not a toy, the
real thing, something that can pierce
hearts…something propelled by
breath, swift and direct, something
to shoot right through the armor,
something to use on journeys when the
going gets rough, something that leaves
a small puncture wound, not a toy,
some kind of deal used to control
large domestic animals, use it in the
city, use it in the country, not a
toy, functonal at the conference
table, a necessity on short trips, not
a toy,
time to build a survival weapon.

HOLY LAND

I want the earth to last
I want it to last beyond Saturday night
and the onion soup
Out beyond walks in the hills
among wild poppies and black dogs
Past Crusader castles and the Jordan River
past Arab guns and Jewish stubbornness
Through rivers and eucalyptus trees
and white horses standing in tall yellow clover
I want the earth to last

HOLY DAYS & BLESSINGS

Our neighbors
Line the wall with faralitos
We light our candles

—Miriam Sagan
HANNUKA

Miriam Sagan

ANTELOPE SEASON

We arrived at night
Driving in rain across the pass
From Raton, New Mexico to Trinidad, Colorado.
The street was empty, dark hilly neighborhood
That spoke of mines
Opening and closing,
A drop in the price of silver.
Temple Aaron on erev Rosh Hashana,
Stone synagogue, built in 1883
With a red wooden cupola
Perched on its roof
Like a rakish hat on a plump lady.

Entering the shul
My eyes flooded with tears,
That smell—incense, furniture polish, wax, desire,
Despair, hope, prayers of childbirth, and cancer,
Bankruptcy, new love, and lost land.
We sat on velvet cushions
In a congregation of only thirty
We could not have felt more far-away
In Shanghai, or Lima.
We were the only Jews
Between Denver and El Paso.

Stained glass windows
Reached from floor to ceiling
An abstract pattern of blue and orange.
My daughter pressed her nose against a pane
Inside each colored square
A mysterious fire was dancing
Double helix glittering and moving
I could find no source
To that trick of light

That kept dancing.

I recited the prayer for the dead, my dead,
That puzzling prayer, Kaddish,
Which offers no consolation
But the praise of God.
Yellow lines of the highway led me here.
Redwing blackbirds flocked
Antelopes grazed
By the side of the road among sunflowers and chamisa.
It was antelope season in these days
Of awe when the hinge swings
Between earth and heaven
Days that run quickly
Hoofs pounding
The dust of plains we call home.

Barbara Rockman

EREV ROSH HASHONA

We enter the synagogue at night, grown-ups
letting our children play out front.
Small ones chase around the building,
while young teens hunt cigarettes and marijuana.

Inside, the Rabbi will describe the new year
beneath the tiled Star of David,
beneath Hebrew letters that spell *Shalom*.
Do we all want to know how we arrived here?
Our kids would rather shiver in circles on the steps
than come in to the stuffed room of chant and parent.
As we read from The Gates of Repentance,
its gilt pages and Hebrew prayers like
braille of the disenfranchised, even the Rabbi
admits some here don't believe in God.

I am one of the women decked in pearls,
while outside the stars pierce
a sky like the roaches of joints
we once inhaled from burnt thumbs and flicked
the last flash into the air. I'm trying to retrace a flight
from home so long ago I can't find the right exit visas
or addresses I've left behind, the lost trail
from 1968 to middle class. All that belief
in Be Here Now and Own Nothing
the family years have blurred.

Outside, my daughter,
who is beautiful and shy, mouths nineties lingo of friends
with an animal instinct for camouflage, the way I lean
tense in my chair to hear every word of prayer,
gut wrenching cries of the Cantor. I want
to belong, the same way my daughter is out
in the halo of lit windows, in the cold
echo of ancient songs wanting to say,
"I am here," in a way that will not make her
a stranger to everyone she wants to love her.

Joan Logghe

TASHLICH AT EMBUDO CROSSING

Tashlich is performed after the Rosh Hashana morning service.
Pieces of bread are cast onto moving water as we name our sins as
part of the ten days of purification during the Days of Awe.

I yell "Negativity!" fling bread
Into the Río Grande, Rosh Hashana
This year, 5757, year of drought, loss,
Too many young deaths. Rare rainy

Afternoon, three menopausal women
Scanning our bodies, our tapped hearts
For what has missed the mark.
We call them sins. Turn from each other

Searching our core. "Lust, greed,
Lack of discipline!" Flag of my ego, shards
Of braided bread. "Passivity, hard heartedness."
We scour our crannies for crumbs, throw

Sin into forgiving current. Downstream
Three strangers shoot a roll of film.
Capturing while we, for now, release.
The Río Grande always was a prayer.

The river washes, washes, a giant tear.
Picture Moses lifted. Picture the Sea
Of Reeds, all that water has been made to bear.
Teshuvah means turn inward.

Ask for inscription in a holy year.
Lately the years hold lessons we've come
To fear. We dip apples in honey for sweetness,
Ask to be inscribed in the Book of Life.

We fling the last piece in silence, naming
To ourselves what we won't frame
In the chosen air. We try and hold back
Nothing from the river. Emptier, we leave.

Drive south. Good medicine of river. God
Who knows about turning, noise into silence,
Air into bird, water into fish,
Takes these morsels and makes a river in us.

Barbara Rockman

THOUGHTS AT KOL NIDRE

Driving to temple, two
rainbows cross the sky.
Sun lifts from the crevice
between mountains, like dew
rising between breasts.

We say *head of the year*:
a clearing to pray.

In the cool pews
you close your eyes
next to the woman who clutches
her handkerchief in thick-veined hands
and cries.

We may or may not
meet God.

All the times you've reached
for grace, the serene
pool of still water:

Once you inhaled the echo of a bronze gong.
How you wanted the radiant third eye.

Once you slept beneath her paisley shawl
and hoped for your grandmother's
fingers on your cheek.

Do we dream we'll wake,
our palms filled with gold sand?

Even as we part the branches
over a familiar trail
aren't we longing for music
we heard before birth?

But none of this may happen.

Sitting in rows, bent on devotion
you may see the shopping list or
fat rain suck at the window.

You may hear the man nearby
clear his throat. Trucks shift gear.

You may recall smells of split oranges,
the carrot pulled from dirt.

Still, the shofar exhales
its long arc of yearning.

You turn to the woman,
her tears cleared:
this common ground.

DAYS OF AWE

Cried next to a woman I just met
during the Days of Awe. And this
was a year not so many bad things
happened that you could fill
your shopping bag with clouds.

The moon is shaped like a coin.
The earth like a cup. I go on
pouring the light into the dark,
the shadow into the eyes, my child
into her destiny.

Marketplaces sell and sell, a thousand
years they go on moving goods
from hand into heart into mouth
into hand. The tongue goes on moving
love from person to person, as a clock moves time.

I want the poems the women of India spoke
in Sanskrit, to enter my bedroom
with the light from the minted moon.
My dreams filled the house with black statues
lining the walls, black angels and saints.

My dream brought love with a black stranger.
His name is "Never Mind." Ten days between
New Year and Atonement on the calendar.
All the women look into their brocade hearts
and put their holiday shoes away.

At week's end, the shoes are filled
with fish and tears. The sins that float
away on bits of bread have been eaten
by white feathered ducks, dissolved, as if
cloud is a sin shifting from land to sky.

The woman and the child are waxed clean.
Polished like Sanskrit, translated into eternity.
Their words hammered into impermanence and shed
and shed, like tears, like prayers, like skins,
like sins, like the heart itself knocked open.

The Torah contains, like a sage, wrapped babe
all the letters from the genes, messages
only a few can walk right into. The holidays
are ten days shaped in one breath. "Rachim."
The word for womb and compassion are the same.

Awe. Say awe.
God points a light down your throat.
Open your mouth to God.

Robin Becker

YOM KIPPUR, TAOS, NEW MEXICO

I've expanded like the swollen door in summer
       to fit my own dimensions. Your loneliness

is a letter I read and put away, a daily reminder
       in the cry of the magpie that I am

still capable of inflicting pain
       at this distance.

Like a painting, our talk is dense with description,
       half-truths, landscapes, phrases layered

with a patina over time. When she came into my life
       I didn't hesitate.

Or is that only how it seems now, looking back?
       Or is that only how you accuse me, looking back?

Long ago, this desert was an inland sea. In the mountains
       you can still find shells.

It's these strange divagations I've come to love: mid-day sun
       on pink escarpments; dusk on grey sandstone;

toe-and-finger holes among the three-hundred and fifty-seven foot
       climb to Acoma pueblo, where the spirit

of the dead hovers about its earthly home
       four days, before the prayer sticks drive it away.

Today all good Jews collect their crimes like old clothes
       to be washed and given to the poor.

I remember how my father held his father around the shoulders
     as they walked to the old synagogue in Philadelphia.

"We're almost there, Pop," he said. "A few more blocks."
     I want to tell you that we, too, are almost there,

for someone has mapped this autumn field with meaning, and any day
     October, brooding in me, will open to reveal

Our names—inscribed or absent—
     among the dry thistles and spent weeds.

Judith Rafaela

ATONEMENT SONGS

I am wild for wild things:
Speech sounds, words running across my mind,
Tastes of sweetness on the tongue,
And I'm wild about
brain chemistry and models of learning.
And sounds.
Tones, timbre, pitch, rhythm
I have music in my genetic structure.

The wild sound of the shofar
pierces my skin and opens my heart.
And I'm wild for tunes in a minor key
that vibrate my tailbone and belly
and echo out across a synagogue packed
with doubters and believers
who come together in whiteness
one day of the year to hear
archaic bizzare legal formulas and prayers.
Sexist, racist, but still...
Dressed up in sounds they open our path.
Just for that moment in our fasting, light-headedness,
open us to rich tones—
Simple melodies that convey truths or fictions
about our fate.
We have free choice, but yet
our fate is sealed this Wednesday night at sundown.

I'm wild about the sun going down and I'm starving and
the gates of heaven are closing
and there's just few minutes.
Wait, don't close.
Wait for my prayer. I'll be better.
Forgive me. Next year. Wait.

Reduced to childlike quaking, we sing incantations
from an earlier time:
three times Baruch Shem
seven times Adonai Hu Elohim and then,
and then the piercing longed for
wail of pain blown up to the heavens
it's getting dark, and
seven Amens.

Carol Moldaw

LINES BEGUN ON YOM KIPPUR
For Yehudis Fishman

1.
I picture you in a phone booth
as you say your mid-day prayer,
the receiver a prop in your hand.

No one pays any attention
except God, who accepts all charges,
always pleased to be called.

Now, picture me in full lotus,
amid a mandala of crystals,
in front of a burning candle.

If, as you say, this—
our earth—is God's basement,
then that explains the clutter

of co-existence, the profusion
of road maps, the pamphlets
and mislabled boxes, but why

is it some of us rummage madly
while others sort through one crate
with infinitesimal care?

2.
In that room, I followed Innana down
and hung by my toes from a thorn tree;

I lay on my back watching the stars
inside the dome of my mother's womb;

I pulled at the gold and silver threads
in her green sari until they snapped;

I followed the dissolving clouds of my breath
but soon they amassed and darkened;

I lay drenched and stunned in that downpour;
I was pelted by stones yanked from my own pocket;

I left myself to die.
I walked to the window.

In a building across the way,
I saw some old men praying at Shul.

They were wearing skullcaps and tallisim.
Each held a prayer book to his breast.

I watched through my curtain while they davened,
bobbing and swaying to greet the Sabbath Queen.

3.
You taught me that the word, in Hebrew,
generates and, by its emanations,
keeps the world in existence;
that each verse in the Book of Lamentations
begins with a different letter,
so that there is an end to suffering.

You said the high should reach down
to elevate the low; that before the Fall,
Adam and Eve had bodies of light,
and, had they waited for the Sabbath,
sanctified, they could have had their fruit.
You said that nothing's so holy and open

as the open rift in a broken heart;
that miracle is catastrophe's correlative.
You said sleep contains a 60th, 'a touch,'
of death; Torah, a touch of Heaven;
Sabbath, Paradise; and dreams, prophecy.
As for poetry…that, you've left up to me.

4.
To hear the long and short piercing blasts
of the shofar, I sneaked into a synagogue
a few blocks from my house one Rosh Hashanah.
The service was almost over, so I slipped past
the men in dark suits that guard both doors,
as if I'd just been out stretching my legs.
I was wearing a dress my mother would approve of,
and I found an empty seat right on the aisle.
I even thought of joining that congregation,
but to me, the rabbi in his tall furred hat,
his white embroidered fur-trimmed flowing robe,
looked more like some kind of priest than a rabbi.
Could I, over time, have made up the censer and smoke
that seems closer in spirit to the Holy Ghost
than to the ghastly fumes from the Holocaust?
The cantor's voice filled out the airy dome.
I heard the longed-for sweet and raspy blasts,
then took a walk to the river before going home.

At the river, I leaned over the wooden piling.
Anchor lines clanked against houseboats and piers.
Pulling some cracker crumbs out of my pocket,
I cupped them against the wind in the palm of my hand.
Like errands, my sins easily slip my mind,

but I compiled a list from odds and ends
guessed at or remembered; it was years ago now,
but how much do categories of sins change?
You might lie to yourself one year, your spouse another;
have greed for money, power, greed for fame;
be vain about looks, or just be generally vain....
Gossiping's like a cold that runs its course,
no matter how you try to avoid it. Like envy,
it's hard to shake, but that year, I remember,
I took envy by its anorexic waist
and threw it into the river and watched it drown,
though the crumbs themselves floated in a cluster,
unspiraling as the current sped them away.

Yehudis Fishman

SUKOS QUARTET

The golden Esrog
weathers all seasons,
swaying with the pulse of time.

The Lulav's fronds
refuse to open,
until prayer is done.

The three-leaved myrtle
radiates everlasting life
from Shabos scents.

In mutual lowliness,
the willows bow and weep
on each other's shoulders.

Phyllis Hotch

SUKKOT: HARVEST DANCE

yesterday
when they
were dancing on the grass
    high desert sky deep
               blue
      around them
dresses and shirts
      bright white
      aqua and black
in a circle
    men women
      boys
         girls
pulling in
pulling out
foot across
foot behind
    stamp to the right
    step step

oh they were
twisting turning together

and the little girl laughing
laughing
    she could not remember
to lift her feet
in the happy sun

people
so beautiful when they dance

CHANUKA

Children mirrored in a dark window
reach to light candles
tall and small in line
Songs dance above the flames,
Songs of a miracle in
Ladino, Yiddish, English
They turn and turn to music
from a shtetle across a faraway sea.

Two big frying pans,
latkes in peanut oil,
not frybread not sopapillas in lard.
Bottles of sweet wine, platters of cakes,
piles of pennies on the floor
and a dreidle carved by a santero
who shrugged as he cut a piece
of the story into each side.

All on the floor with the children
Tewa, Taoseño, and mestizo Jews
twirling a wooden dreidle—
a miracle in each face.

Joan Logghe

SHALOM SHALOM

Light forty-four candles
it's that season again,
when money and love flow thin
and clean and wild as a trout stream.
I want to splash it all over,
stretch it eight days like temple oil
in the everlasting light.

Six stars of peace and one more candle.
Love is rarefied in mountain air,
inhaled like a day without a shopping list.

Christmas Eve it's the fourth night,
Light me four candles.
Shalom, Shalom.
Stay quiet till it's wick and wax,
then one by one they're out.

In the morning the house is electric
with children from two worlds early,
earth and sky, dreams and tiptoes
on top of the stairs,
asking, "Just one present now?"

We nod yes, reluctant to leave our bed
and see it all end,
father Christmas and the Channuka woman,
overlapping in flannels.

PURIM

The night of Purim
My daughter dresses carefully
Pink leotard, pink tights, gold lace
Ballet slippers, voile tutu,
Pink satin cape, crown
Of ribbons and rosebuds
Scepter of silver glitter
Lipstick, no sweater.
She is Queen-Esther-who-saves-the-Jews
I am more ambiguous
Green eyeshadow, a wig
Of purple beads with Cleopatra bangs
Regular mother dress, and pink
Feather boa I've lifted from her dresser.

Recently, out walking in Galisteo
With two friends in March mud
Under the sign of Pisces I tell the story: how Vashti
Refuses to dance naked
For her husband the king
At a party. My friends
Shake their heads, both lovely
Middle-aged, grey hair, and gentle
Say, they say simultaneously
"I'd have gone to dance."
Half-wishing someone would request
We'd shake our booties
Like G-string girls, we laugh
At something in ourselves
Head for river's cedar banks.

I'd like to write the alphabet
A hundred and one times in the shape of my body
I'd like to be Vashti
In purple beads I bought
On a whim, young and broke
Coveting harem.
But my daughter puts me
In my place, says firmly
As we head for shul:

       Mommy, I am Queen Esther
       And you, mom
       Are just Queen Esther's mother.

Annah Sobelman

COOKING *HAMANTASCH*

When I really wanted to
speak, she started making the interesting *hamantaschen* pastries. Birds

were coming out, too, not

speechless, starting to sing with even more dark whistle authority
since the *hamantaschen* tries to open up our mouths

when we get shut
in them. These birds were *black interrogatory*

upon black. These birds were *that throat sometimes inside pounding with*
the beaks

by which *in*
Odessa my heart

inside winter harsh sounds gets stuck. By which she heard nightly

on the shores *bereaving,*
ferocious, steps, through what heart

inside winter would she have to sweep? To which, lighting candles,

triangular *hamantaschen*
fill up with prunes which talk about Esther speaking

loudly to her husband the king about the traitor Hamen in order to warn
        mad Israel
so they would not be without defense. Israel wouldn't stop

talking. *Or open up my old*
stoves, heart of sweating plums. This was to help me. *I'm sweeping*

in order to burn those bridges, she said, shoving out *bird*
black soot, and in fact, with my Jewish mouth, I'm cooking with

her right now in the old Odessa

oven which smells a lot like my
grandma's *sweeping fear arm out in the frost emigrant whoosh*. Were the
        prunes unlike

the rage? Is memory cooking in the

heating prune paste because she couldn't otherwise hold all her bird's hard
whistling? When I start speaking, she puts me

into the interesting
hamantaschen dough trying to get me to chew faster, birds especially

on her thick upper arms where she's sweeping methodically with such *husk-*

accent whisk since my childhood
also sometimes scared me. *I'm shoving living out toward*

plums of birds, she says, since there is still a lot of cooking to
be done above the thick emigrant sheets, meaning sleeping without

safety tears
things. Were the birds unlike the rage? Which

tore through her own feel slower? *Patter patter down the cobbled twilight*

be quiet before
and after dark. Which flew faster down her own nervous

roof? Or she'd say *sometimes I wondered about plucking*

the rowdy plums off their
boughs, but still, if you can, believe in mouths and fortunate

gambling. The violence is done to the plums so the ode to joy won't have to
        stumble down again
I hope, very much—*Oh mouth,*

she'd say, with the good heaviness coming up—*Oh heart,* I'd answer, also

coming up with her from the inside
of the stove since I wanted to get out and eat where the birds

and whisker chins
talk faster, full of tongues of *hamantaschen* and

talkative huge sighs, and since I wanted to also be more tasted—

PASSOVER

Jews must be everywhere
Even in La Puebla, New Mexico
Where we pass Good Friday pilgrims
Wearing walkmans
Dusty along the highway
It's shabbos, the two sets of candles
Adorn the tables
Set with sea shells
Seder means: the order
In which things happen
Egypt means: narrows
For plagues we dip our fingers in the wine
Hail kills your tomato plants
You quarrel
With a neighbor about a wall
A friend is unexpectedly in jail
Baby cries in the emergency room
Homeless men sleep in the arroyo
Stumble across Paseo to the liquor store
So drink four cups of wine
It's only the second time this year
Jews must get drunk
And lie down with our shoes off
On comfortable couches
The children are playing in the dusk
My daughter feeds a large white horse
A bunch of golden apples
Desert smells like the sea
Of sand and wind and something else
Clean, and scoured
Miriam's Well

Springs within
Green oasis that must
Reappear within our hearts
Voices singing slightly off-key
This source of water
Follows us
Despite our exile, wandering.

Shuli Lamden

FOUR QUESTIONS

Now that I am grown, now
that my brother presides over Seder in his own home,
now that my seven-year-old nephew has outgrown the asking
and coaches his little sister in the questions, word by word—

> *Why is tonight different from all other nights?*
> *How is this meal different from all other meals?*

—only now do I know
not simply answers, but the ways
that our questions are answered,
with still more questions:

> *How is tonight the same as all other nights like this?*
> *How is this meal the same as all other meals like this?*

Dad explains to his grandson
how over and over we sit down to this meal,
how his own grandfather once asked the questions,
then heard them asked.

We begin with memory, tell stories, and sing
of our ancestors and of God who redeems us.
We are always enslaved,
and we are always being liberated.
While the sun burns its way from night to night,
the Red Sea touches shore, then recedes.

Shuli Lamden

SUBURBAN SEDER

Now is the skit,
and my brother plays Moses. He parts the sea
in a yellow chenille bathrobe. He waves a curtain rod,
and darkness falls over the earth.
He gestures again, I switch on the lights,
and my cousins, the children of Israel,
are delivered from slavery.

I open the sliding glass door for Elijah. I know
he will enter. Dad pours him a cup of wine. I wait
for the prophet's invisible lips
to sip from the silver goblet,
for his invisible bones
to recline
among ours.

But look—the matzoh's disappeared!
We search between sofa cushions,
palm the pockets of the pool table, clear out
stereo cabinet, piano bench, every vase on the mantel.
Finally, Dad reveals it's hidden
in the dictionary,
under M.

Dayenu, we sing,
it would have been enough
to be brought out of Egypt, to be given the law.
We dip parsley, green from our own garden.
Somewhere behind this night, the sun burns
like a bush on distant mountains.
The Red Sea touches shore, then recedes.

SHAVUOS

Did the spirit of ha shem
        come down and visit
        the little room
        where we waited
        through the night
for dawn's revelation?

Did angels watch over
        the stained-glass windows of the shul,
        where—over coffee,
        cake and rugelach—
        we pondered the sleep
of our ancestors?

Did the birds,
        rousing us
        from our questions
        and interpretations
        at the sun's purple showing
sing with new inspiration?

And did that light
        that played round my head
        the next day,
        after noon, when I woke,
        arise from someplace
other than the sun?

BLESSINGS

BEFORE FOOD
permission to see more
than colors and shapes.
permission to smell more
than beckoning odors.
permission to taste
from a center
of insatiable yearning.

AFTER FOOD
awe-struck
that You continue
to nourish
long after even I
can no longer discern
the physical presence
of sustenance.

SIX

Wings of prayer, apparently impervious—
ruffled by the slightest
breeze of thought.

Mikvah at dawn—
hovering light plunges,
deep down in waters of Eden.

Marble skies at dawn—
a book falls from the shelf
as yet unopened.

A helicopter hovers.
Stuck in stubborn quicksand!
Prayer waits.

Rabbi Nachman says,
'make prayers from Torah,'
woman's day is coming.

The leaf spirals slowly,
not landing till it cools
a sun-struck worm.

Miriam Sagan

MIKVAH PSALM

Under the cover
Of darkness
Under the cover
Of night
I'm descending backwards
Into the pool
I'm climbing down

Under the cover
Of water, I'm
Letting go three times
Under water
Not touching the walls
Of the floor
Like a child too small
To kick the womb

She holds a towel
I climb the ladder
Out of the water
Water that penetrated
My every
Thought.

Joan Logghe

BLESSING

Dear my heart
maker of mitzvahs on my body
all the earth fills with our blessings
angels all around us for shabbos
holy one of patience and good will
not even God comes this close to me
though you give me tastes of God.
Blessing of the husband, blessing
of the wife. The whole night wine,
and braided and light.

Yehudis Fishman

SHABOS IN SANTA FE

Shabos morning
when the sun whistles
a mild breeze
I begin my forty minute walk
to the only shul in Santa Fe.
I walk with the smell of roasting chilies
and daffodils dancing
in unexpected corners.
Catching my strolling scent,
barking Chows and Dobermans
greet me like a bucket brigade.
I try to tiptoe by the old collie
who is always shedding
and ferociously protective
of her ramshackle paradise.
I don't vary my route very often,
but the changes happen anyway.
Like the hand-made furniture store on Early Street
turning into 'Luvs and Teens Driving School,'
Like gardens and adobes springing up
on last week's barren land,
Like prairie dog holes in the railroad yard
being paved over and rerouted.
Nothing stays the same on my way to shul,
even when I walk precisely
in last week's footsteps.
Nothing but the inevitable penny
that greets me when I happen to look down,
especially on Calle Grillo—an uphill walk
which slows my steps just long enough to notice.
But I cannot stop to pick up pennies
no matter how they glow and beckon.
It is Shabos in Santa Fe
and I am on my way to the house of G-d.

And even if the shul itself would change,
would no longer be a kosher shul,
would no longer house myself
as well as fellow travelers,
I still would not stop for shiny pennies.
It would still be Shabos in Santa Fe,
and I would still be on my way
to the house of G-d.

YA TOMAS TU LUGAR (YOU TAKE YOUR PLACE)
Song for my son, Max, on his Bar Mitzvah

Este ya es el día
en que te vuelves hombre
con apoyo de familia
y de comunidad.

En frente a Dios te pones
con corazón y mente
ahora a estar pendiente
de tu responsabilidad.

Que ya no eres un niño
que esconde en su madre
secretos de ternura
ahora los guardas tú.

Que ya no eres un niño
llorando en la puerta.
Como hombre en el templo
ya tomas tu lugar.

This is the day
in which you become a man
with the support of your family
and your community.

You place yourself in front of God
with heart and mind
ready now
for your responsibility.

For you are no longer a child
who hides in his mother
tender secrets
you now keep them to yourself.

For you are no longer a child
crying at the door.
As a man in the temple
you take your place.

ANCESTORS

The uncle's lopped-off head,
Cossacks in the sister's bed,
and the boy who hid, then fled,
took a name from the river
and crossed the sea, found
Ida, had you—who had me.

—Carol Moldaw
PATRILINEAGE

Rabbi Lynn Gottlieb

WOMEN'S GENEALOGY FROM THE TORAH

Mother Chant

Brucha Ya Shekinah hanotenet orah l'sapair sipurim.

Blessed are you who gives your light

To inspire the telling of sacred tales.

Night Sea Woman   Tehom

Light That Dwells Within Woman   Shekinah

Fiery Night Woman   Lilith

Let There Be Life Woman   Hava

Mother of the Tent Women   Adah

Flute Song Woman   Zilah

Voice of the Flood Woman   Na-amah

See Far Woman   Sarah

Outcast Woman   Hagar

Pillar of Salt Woman   Eshet Lot

Praises All Life Woman   Yehudit

Earth Smelling Sweet Woman   Basmat

Buffalo Woman   Rivkeh

Talking Bee Woman   Devorah

Soft Eyes Woman   Leah

Soft Heart Woman   Rachel

Truth Seeking Woman   Dinah

Desert Eagle Woman   Asnat

Smells of Time Woman   Serach

Horn of Freedom Woman   Shifra

Helping Hand Woman   Puah

Golden Cloud Woman   Yocheved

And never was there a prophet like Miriam HaNavia:

She sang open the waters of the sea,

And all the people passed through to freedom.

T'halelli yah t'halleli ya t'halleli ya t'halleli ya

la la la la la la la la la la la la laa!

UNCLE HYMIE

My Uncle Hymie
cracked his head in Friedrichstadt
and became a natural surrealist.
He would visit us
in the Bronx
and leave a memory
of his presence,
a circle in a Rubik's cube,
a picture no one could recognize.
The last time I saw him
he was wearing a tan suit,
well-pressed,
and a subtle
blue-and-gold tie
pinned to his light-blue shirt
by a rearing silver horse.
Hymie was one of my mother's brothers,
Sam's twin.
He had fallen from a barnloft
when they were three.
Later Sam got married,
became a sculptor,
mostly animals,
while Hymie sold
ladies' foundation garments.
Sometimes it was hard to believe he wasn't right,
but when that last time
he took off his jacket, his tie, shirt, and trousers
to show us the corset he was wearing,
my mother placed a hand
over my young eyes
and told Hymie to behave himself.
I remember this, how this uncle
became my favorite
among four others.

Joan Logghe

ALWAYS AUNT CLARA

Always Aunt Clara
asked
in the Home for the Aged
"many Jewish people
in New Mexico?"
Oy Vay,
what could I say?
Now she's dead,
Oy Olé?

The matzoh ball moon
rises over the Sangre de Cristos
on Friday night
candles at my window
prayers for a life
like noodle pudding.

In the Temple Sisterhood Cookbook
I have recipes marked.
Chopped liver was never
my favorite
goes well
with green chile.

After the Indians
came the Spanish
then Christianity
spread like mayonnaise
After a time came the Jews
bearing bagels.

When next we meet
Aunt Clara
I will come riding
out of this life
on a smoked whitefish
herding kippered herrings
a Jewish rodeo
above the Sangre de Cristos
toward the blue tortilla moon.
Joining you for blintzes
joining Chagall
lighting star candles
chanting
Viva Shalom!
Viva
Shalom!

Marcia Wolff

ASSIMILATION

Great grandmother Matel brought her brass
candlesticks to America, lit the candles
each Friday night. When she died
Grandma Molly put them in her drawer and ate

sweet and sour pork at the Chinese
restaurant on the corner. We moved
to a house with a white painted fence,
green shuttered windows. At holiday

time we decorated our tree with red
glass balls, glittering lights,
and mother displayed the tall
taper holders on the corner of her

mahogany buffet. At dawn on Christmas
morning, I pushed the green chair treeside
and climbed it like I did the pecan tree
out back, but we tumbled, crashed

to the floor. I sat in the aftermath
surrounded by red debris, and the
six-pointed star I had stretched for
was smashed, still out of reach.

Jean Nordhaus

SANTA FE: A JEWISH WIFE   1895

Ceta brings the tray again. Supper.
The rattle of keys in the door means food.
The chime of a spoon against glass, sleep.
Her hand on my forehead, darkness. Fevers
quenched under such cool fingers.

These four walls contain me.
I hurl myself against them,
they do not let go. They hear
me out, do not betray
my confidences. Downstairs

the life of the family goes on.
I hear scraping of chairs on the floor.
Clatter of dishes cleared away. From the kitchen,
floral explosions of Spanish. Footsteps. Talk.

This harsh land with its alien colors,
flowers sheathed in spines,
sky breeding clouds above the sword-
encircled blossom, moving shapes
of menace and embrace.

I think of the land of my childhood,
its rivers and castles, the language I knew there,
lush and green, *du liebes Kind*—
Mother's hands above the candles
as she gave the blessing, little hats of shade
above the flame, light lining her fingers
with ribbons of gold.

Here the earth is red and bare.
Bed. Table. Chair.
A body stripped down to essentials
and a heart still capable of violence.
Valves of thunder. Silhouette of bone and scar.
The nine-branched candelabrum of lightning
and the sudden weeping.

Joan Logghe

MY MOTHER'S SABBATH
for Beti

Last week at Sabbath, same napkin
on same color blond hair, I didn't hate
her praying. I drank it exactly as we gather
light from the candles into our heart.

After the blessing she prayed that our family
be consecrated, not mouthing words, I recognized
the real thing, went on asking that we be patient
with one another. She has been patient.

It took forty years for me to enter the prayer
with her. All those Fridays she stood there alone
with her own mother gone so long. With her faith
burning.

The praying my mother did in childhood
scent of gas in the paraffin, cry of child
in her tears, napkin of torn clothing
on her blond hair, made me squirm.

Embarrassed by sentiment, by her asking.
I didn't know what God had to do with weeping
what her mother dead had to do with Friday
how food could taste as good as Eden.

Lights were turned off after dinner,
candles went about their business of burning out.
That was what I savored, alone with flame
in the late part of the evening.

I chose solitude to work out my findings,
harsh God who allowed little girls who wrote
so honestly to die. Allowed mustached man
to make war, his hands stuffing a train full of girls.

Legs stiff for goose steps. My heart aching
at nine and ten, candles sputtering. My mother
already swearing at the Pirates. Lousy season.
"Damn," she'd say in a loud voice, "Damn."

Richard L. Stevens

(in collaboration with Joan Logghe)

SCHLOMO'S HEAVEN

Schlomo's heaven is sweet like orange candy. There is an ocean and a heated pool and no one walks away from anyone else in anger. The street musicians come when you need them, have a magnificent repertoire, and know exactly when to depart. They accept no gratuities.

There's a medium-sized circus in the corner, two rings, and a tiny opera in heaven's vestibule. There's a stellar cast of bite-sized angels performing Rigoletto and eating ice cream cake, a delicious experience.

Schlomo is surrounded by his favorite cigar-smoking uncles and aunts who were terrific cooks and overstuffed furniture and flying wallets stuffed with money and membership cards to country clubs and jazz clubs and men's clubs. Vases of flowers mambo and little children, distant cousins, crawl aroud making conversation and soliciting magic tricks, which Schlomo is delighted to perform. He is a perfect heavenly host.

Why, at evening, is Schlomo sweeping the streets, tidying up Paradise? It is his nature to contribute, make a nice welcome for the next fellow.

Annah Sobelman

MY ODESSA

No, maybe not a shadow,
my grandma Sarah would say, tired of seeing them everywhere, and

anyway she is what

she was in life, many faces, but, picture this, none of them moons
        exactly hanging
over mine. *Those forests were bright flesh inside*

night inside—All along they'd been
shrinking but it's not as if fright alone were seizing them. *You are*
        the violin

almost all of which cuts

into my shoulders, face, my two temples, and *Shtetls near Odessa*
the softness around me

stinks. It made me want to

shrink. For example, *pardon my italics,* or *I didn't mean to shiver*
this extra house, I attributed importantly to her

face inside Russia which felt large but also dwindling on top of
        her shoulders, her body
hung *over* my insides and then *inside* my

air as if she were the drawing
back of a prayer into the breath

of the wood because I thought I heard the bark of the singing trees

sigh. *It's not a curse,*

I said, explaining, as I know them, physics and science as a kind
of elliptical genetic dash and still softer

95

bits of strong violet
white stuff. *Beautiful horses were also in it, lights through the forest,*
    you are my long

waist and shrinking
grandma neck. In her mouth her dazzling shoulders and neck

lest anyone should break
them when they saw her. *Arguably,*

measurably, my body's been taking up less and less of the air. And to the
    thin white

skin notched with dark
brown fright hunching

where the birch were cut, my beloved old ones, also backing me up in
an important forest filled

with miles and miles of freight, I'm trying to
lean forward more than a

soft tongue inside a horse's bit since I think I can grow two, maybe
    three bodies

bigger across danger up
to the train-cutting-through-

them mountains—they're the Urals, horses firm—and then of course
    beyond

these mountains
since I think it's very

important to break the necks of soft houses with our shoulders—

Judyth Hill

ADVICE FROM NANA

Always wear your clothes like they have only been yours.
And never pay retail unless it's divine.
Eat only what you want on your plate and leave anything.
Eat dessert and hors d'oeuvres and skip the entrees, just enjoy.
Make men buy you presents, and if you don't like their taste,
teach them what you love.
If you can't teach them what you love, leave them.
And darling, don't pick your split ends.
Look into the eyes of the person you are talking to
and they will believe you.
If you want to stop someone from criticizing you,
let your chin quiver just a bit, eyes fill up, yes,
there, that's it.

Don't stand in the corner at a party, walk over to the books
and enjoy them, because at least that's fun.
And you should never be uncomfortable at a party, God forbid.
You are so gorgeous.
Remember I love you.
Remember to call me and tell me everything.
Remember this pearl necklace is yours, and the china.
Don't sit with your legs apart,
you're sure to get the wrong boyfriends that way, I surely did.
I had to be told a hundred times too.
Did I tell you I love you?
Lord, you look like your mother at that age, and she was a wild one,
I had my hands full with her, at least you got her brains.
Thank God for that, she was a wiz.

Now remember, if someone asks your name more than three times,
Forget them! Don't tell them!
I never would and I met everyone I needed to.
When you want to know a good restaurant in a strange town,
don't ask at the hotel, just walk a bit, read the menus,
and smell the air when you walk in.
You can always tell by the smell.
And Darling, even a good man can be picked that way...
I always found good men by their smell.

Judyth Hill

MRS. NOAH PEELS POTATOES IN FOUR WORLDS

Who closed the door on Noah's Ark?
Answer: God
—Question posed on "Hollywood Squares"

She is deluged.
She needs an Ark.
Make it of cypress, make it pitch.
She needs two of everything,
and seven of what's really good.

She can handle all those finicky guests that stay and stay.
A family of picky eaters, impossible manners,
beds for every kind of back.
Someone's always hungry, and the cleaning!

She's the perfect hostess.
Learns every song for rainy weather.
A joke for every species of trouble.
This is her chance to start fresh.

Send out a raven!
Send out a dove!
She'll know when it's over.
Knows that when we lose everything,
It's what remains that counts.

In clouds of curling cumulus,
a covenant of color waits.
Adon Olam, close the door.
Let it rain!

Judyth Hill

ANGELS AND THORNS

The first part is about angels.
Wings. Lots of air...
You know how that is. Or do you?
Then there's the thorns.
We know that. The piercing.
The erotic edge.
The touch of harm.
Then that flutter.
Air and rescue,
Wind and the swift descent.
But Jacob, Jacob saw them on the ladder.
And remember, they were going up and coming down.
He knew to build the Temple there.
Because that's where it was.

SNOWED-IN

It is snowing.
A natural chance to be alone
A chance to be with the old
Hasidic masters,
A chance to learn.

It is snowing.
No place to go.
Eating steamed potatoes
And traveling in time and space
Back to Poland and Ukraine.

It is silent in the mountains.
No modern frames of reference.
Snow piled on branches,
Books piled on tables,
Rebbes teaching the mysteries
To peasants.

Carol Moldaw

REB SHMERL AND THE WATER SPIRIT
A Hasidic Tale

Reb Shmerl, a peddler from Constantine,
thought he had found a way to sin
and keep his yearly slate as clean
as clouds, the suds God washes in.

He grabbed up sins at all his stops,
carted them home without a thought,
tossed them down the cellar steps,
slammed the door, and let them rot.

Shmerl raked up his sins each fall,
and stuffed them in a burlap sack
he rolled down to the lake, a ball
that sank like lead. The lake turned black.

"What does it matter?" he would say,
his hawker's hands thrown open wide,
as if to supplicate or pray.
"Whether I toss my sins aside,

or sink them in a capacious lake,
God magnanimously forgives."
He swallowed hard, two gulps, to take
his pieties like sedatives.

So sins, like gold coins, multiplied.
The once-clear lake, the dumping ground,
with black polluted spittle cried
and vowed someone would turn up drowned.

Reb Shmerl had only one regret:
his faithful wife could not conceive
what he somehow could not beget—
no son tugged at his woolen sleeve.

One day he walked from dawn to dusk
carting neither his toys nor tools.
He sought the Baal Shem Tov to ask
if there was any truth to the tales

that he could intercede with God
and grant a pair so old a son.
(Shmerl's wife had given him the glad
thought to turn to this holy man.)

The Master pitied the peddler's wife:
"You'll have a boy, and that is all."
"What more have I asked my entire life?"
The Master stood. Shmerl felt ill.

"Remember this. Thirteen years
he'll grow, strong and swift as an otter.
On his birthday that year, as he is yours,
be sure he doesn't go near water,

or waves will carve your son's coffin
before he prays in synagogue.
Each year you've poisoned the lake with sin
and now it foams like a rabid dog.

That morning when you dress yourself
you'll put two socks on your left foot..."
("The Master's cracked," Shmerl smirked to himself,
blinking his eyes, tapping his feet)

"By your bare foot, recall these words,
and remember to keep your son inside."
The Baal Shem Tov was good as his word:
their son was strong and steady-eyed,

everybody's favorite boy.
He liked to play all day at the lake,
riding on turtles, shouting "ahoy,"
or swimming, with fish flanking his wake.

The boy's Bar Mitzvah day was hot.
Early that morning his father woke
puzzled by a dream he forgot
entirely—like a half-heard joke.

Getting dressed, he began to fume
over a sock he couldn't find.
Searching he hopped around the room,
but anger and effort struck him blind.

Finally, he shook his wife from sleep.
Her laughter like a town crier's bell
gathered neighbors in like sheep
to watch her husband before he fell.

"Where have you put my sock?" he cried.
"You've put them both on your left foot!"
She pointed—the townsmen, crowded inside,
all nodded at Shmerl's wobbling foot.

"I've WHAT?" he snapped, and the key turned
in its lock, the door swung open wide,
and the Master's words that he had spurned
rushed over him like a swelling tide

that rising knocked him down and seized
his heart, his son. His son. Was he
the only boy who had not squeezed
his way into the room to see

Shmerl fall? Shmerl's boy had overslept—
the scorching sun had woken him
with nothing on his mind except
the urge to take his morning swim.

As he ran past his father's door,
Shmerl saw him go and sprang to his feet,
scurried to catch him, begged, then swore,
but the boy raced on and crossed the street.

Shmerl called on God as his son slipped
on the slick grass and fell headlong,
his ankle throbbing, a tendon ripped.
"Get back inside, where you belong."

Shmerl gripped his arm to lead him home
and shouldered him like a sack of sins
until the boy stood up on his own,
Shmerl all the while muttering *Amens*.

The boy was locked in his room all day.
He begged, but was forbidden water.
Worn-out, unable to get his way,
he slept and dreamt he swam in water

clear as glass and marble-cool.
He dreamt he grew enormous fins.
As guardian of the swimming hole,
he wasn't scared of the old man's sins.

By noon, heat made it hard to breathe.
Most villagers were down at the lake
when the water started to swirl and seethe—
boats were capsized in the quake,

but no one saw the spirit rise
until it thrust its hands in the air.
Black tears fell from its red-rimmed eyes.
Seaweed hung from its head like hair.

It searched from face to face before
any had time to reach the bank.
All heard its voice, like thunder, roar
"One is missing." And then it sank.

Watching his son's long sleep, Shmerl saw
the water spirit rise and claim
his boy as forfeit under the law
for the slew of sins that bore his name.

He knew them well and denied none,
repenting each, from first to last.
At midnight, when Shmerl woke his son,
the boy was hungry from his fast

and his ankle throbbed, but he was safe.
Shmerl's wife prepared the feast and set
an extra place by the large carafe—
the Baal Shem Tov would join them yet.

HAVING A WONDERFUL HOLIDAY

Palm Springs, Jan 9th.
　　　I'm as comfortably settled
as a flower girl at a mock wedding...
I always hear you.
After I left the Holy Land I spent
days in Istanbul listening to
white doves.
The Greeks have their own sounds.
River Nile, Feb 24th.
Will you tell Willard, I'll be home
before long.
The Alhambra is beautiful.
　Leaving for Madrid
　　　　to pick up the car and on to
　　　　Paris.
The tides are quite remarkable.
At low tide the water goes out
for ten miles. At high tide it comes in
ten miles. In ten minutes, a wall of
water...
　　　　Photo Velours, Fabrication
　　　　Francaise...
Sent you a telegram from El Paso.
Which I hope you received.
Sent you a card from San Antonio.
The trip was long and the altitude
is not very good either...
Vista Panoramica, Colour Natural
Having a wonderful holiday in Paris,
Kit and Chick are fine, having a drink
with them in an hour. Leaving for
Florence tonight. Greetings from the
Eiffel tower...Pisa, April 24th. A remarkable sight.
179 feet high and fourteen feet out of perpendicular...

Bill Gersh

JUST ANOTHER MUMMY IN THE CARGOE

Dancing together on the golden
streets of glory.....
transformed into their heavenly
bodies.. yiddish cries muffled
in leaky sprinkler systems..

Voices of Russian ancestors move
from air conditioner to air
conditioner. White winged aluminum
hurls through Miami skies.

Watching my hands reach for light
I see this is the animal, the
sacrificial creature, the animal
the ancestor, the ancestor of tongue,
the giver of lot for able,
       animal of the word
       of speaking peoples
       of the ram, of the linga
       of the reason for line
I kid thee not daddy, i kid thee
not.. there for endless horizon
miles ..clothed mummies had risen
from the cargoe of unknowns..
stretched elongations encased in
stainless steel screaming with voices of Russian ancestry.

KADDISH

The mourning doves sit shivah
on Lama Mountain, out of respect
the clouds cover the pond.

—Joan Logghe
from ONE WILD JEW MISSING

GRAPES FROM THE FISHMAN

No one has asked me about her for so long.
When the Neumans walked in my bakery
I said, My mother bought our fish from you when I was growing up.
I told him my maiden name
and he said, Of course, you're Suzanne's daughter.
How is your mother?
October is her 6 year Yahrzeit I say,
It's hard he says, tears in his eyes and his wife hugs me.
Later, they return, with green grapes.

No one has said her name to me for so long.

Suddenly she is real, and I would call her for the new year.

L'Shana Tovah Mom, four grandchildren, God is good, no?
and we could schmooz, I would promise her pictures and forget to
    send them.
Where are my new pictures of you and the kids she'd say,
you never sent them and did you call your grandmother for the yontif
and wasn't the weather beautiful for the holidays this year.
It always is, God makes fall just for Jews.
And how's your weight, pumpkin?
I hope you're not bigger, you're alright now, but…and such a pretty face.

The great Yiddishe secret: How did we all get pretty faces
    and big tushes?

Mom is dead and that is not a secret.

It's in the air on the holy days, the weather of longing,
of blessings and sorrow.
But Mr. Neuman brought me grapes,
grapes for his memories of her, for my memories of her.
Fall and those few deciduous trees that do turn in the desert,
and the Kaddish I will say for her at Yiskor, this and all my years.
And the tears for that moment,
salty, burning, like the fiery tips of poplars,
memories that flame, that catch and spread,
the sting of autumn, aspens on the cusp of winter,
and sweet too,
grapes from the fishman, her name in conversation.

A WIDOW'S KADDISH

Standing behind the screen
Listening to the minyan of men
I stand up and say kaddish
For my dead husband
That ladder of prayer
Aramaic with rungs of Hebrew

A prayer like smoke
Or a well-worn pathway
Ancient Polynesian trail on the Na Pali Coast
Stones worn smooth by passing feet
Or handholds in Frijoles Canyon
Scooped from tuff to the mesa top

Lines on the palm—
Lines on the map—
Neither prepared me for the terrain itself
Lifeline ends
Luminous monitor goes flat
Your heart fails
The weeping nurse
Disconnects you
From respirator that fills your lungs
With artificial air.

Arm of the starfish
Leg of the salamander
Neural pathway
That can rejuvanate
I'll drink a shot of schnapps
L'Chaim—
It's late at night
We're getting a little drunk
Jupiter is hanging
Brilliant object above the shul's parking lot
I go home singing
In the dark.

Phyllis Hotch

KADDISH FOR DEBBIE 1951–1997

My daughter was buried
near the ocean
under a fringe of green spruce
>   *Yisgadal*

Each morning
when the sun rises
in the notch
between these peaks,
I pray
>   *viyiskadash*

The tips of my shoes
touch the edge
of her deep grave
>   *vimru omayn*

Her pine coffin
becomes her pine crib
>   *olmayo*

Her arms raise to me
>   *Yisborach*
to lift her
>   *valkol yisroel*

I nod to her
>   *hu ya seh shalom*

and pray
>   *shalom alaynu*

for the peace in the infinite sky

Shuli Lamden

JEWISH IMAGERY

There is always a desert and a cemetery.
Sometimes the two are the same. Once,
backpacking through Big Bend, David and I
came upon a pioneer's cemetery. No Jews,

only a few rotted wooden crosses. Out there
so little to brighten the slight mounds of graves
that survivors bent daisy shapes with barbed wire
and planted their twisted stems in the hard white earth.

No wonder we leave stones.
I don't suppose there were flower shops in the Sinai
when Moses and his followers bent to dig
and cover graves during those forty years.

My father, born not far from here in arid Colorado,
says he has no memories
before those of his father's funeral. 1927, Denver,
everything a bleak snowstorm. "We drove way out of town on Colfax,"

he tells me before I fly up to Denver and find the grave.
I find the house too, and Dad's elementary school,
but the Queen of Angels orphanage across the street
is now a Motel 6 and a Burger King.

When I show Dad the photos, I can coax a few more images
out of him...the way the cat cowered underneath the couch
during summer thunderstorms, skating in winter on Rocky Mountain
Lake.
But ask him outright, and Dad will always say

he remembers nothing before his father's funeral.
I never thought to ask what he does remember of that day,
but I found out inadvertently, as we planned my brother's funeral.
When it was his turn to take a handful of earth

and throw it on his father's coffin, my Dad,
only nine, took fright and ran away. He hid,
even now he won't say where.
Somehow reunited with his mother and brother,

he went to his first Seder that night
at the home of a stranger named Ida Katz.
The next morning they got up, went to the train station,
and boarded a train for California.

SISTER

Just this last June we were in Milwaukee together, playing
tennis, going to the sand dunes on Lake Superior. We ate at
Benjamin's delicatessen everyday.

But most I remember her in the haunted dark train station, a
paper bag at her feet full of strawberries and melons. She sat
in that thin wood chair with her long hair, face almost like
mine, fuller mouth. There's always one in the family more
beautiful: you give that gift to them and go on.

She sat there sad. She knew I would take the long train up along
the Mississippi into Minnesota. I'd take it alone and we'd
sit in two separate Midwest cities, neither of us having found
our way out of the circle of family in New York, the Sunday
dinners and death of our grandfather. Neither of us would
quite make it through the white clouds of America.

She sat and sighed and at least 500,000 Jewish women in train
stations all over Europe did the same thing not so many years ago.

JUDYTH HILL

STAR CHILDREN

In Holland, they say, the trains always ran on time.
The trains, they said, always ran on time.
I could say it slower, though you know I speak quickly.
I could say it quietly, but it's screaming in my heart.

In Holland, they say, they were good to their Jews.
The Juden, they say.

They consented, they say, to putting stars on the children,
the Star of David, a yellow star,
constellations of the innocent ones
on trains that always ran on time.

They were good to their Jews, they say,
allowed a bit of normalcy, and perhaps an older woman would
                    brush the hair
of the younger starry ones, or soothe them to sleep,
or rock the little yellow starred ones,
that slept to the whistle of the trains that ran on time.

She was a star child too, but the star was not yellow
and it was not pinned to a blue wool sweater.
The trains here ran on time also.

Her mother would take her and her little sister
to sit in Penn Station on 34th Street.

She would buy them Jujubes, and they would rest their legs,
rocking their little luggage back and forth.
There was nowhere to go,
and the conductor would call the times of the trains
that ran through to these impossible late night elsewheres.
Have I told you that the ceiling there is made of stars,
of all the constellations and of two small girls
at their mother's feet in a train station going absolutely
                    nowhere,
under these stars, the children closed their eyes
and went there.

LISTEN CAREFULLY

You don't want to hear it.
The sound of glass breaking in eleven hundred synagogues.
You don't want to hear it,
Treblinka, Dachau, Auschwitz, Bergen-Belsen.
You don't want to hear it, and I don't want to tell it,
but I do, over and over, the names and the glass crashing
into cobbled streets in a very young Germany in 1938.
Fifty years I say.
Don't you say. Don't say it.
The world knew I say
Someone must have heard the fires as they roared up aisles,
burning the mehitzah, burning the bimah,
licking the velvet curtain of the aron kodesh,
and finally the Torah ablaze, crumbing to ash,
our scrolls so holy we are afraid to touch them,
make laws for the law.
Our holiest ablaze in the shattering dark.
It was night, and the butcher and baker and candlestick maker
became ashes, ashes, and we all fell down.

You don't want to hear it.
I try not to hate. I don't even hate, actually.
These days I think of sirens and alarms.
I answer all calls, all letters.
I'll respond to any summons, say Yes I'm here
and I know. I remember. I want to remember.
I want to remember to remember the past,
I want to name all the extinct species.
I want to remember the trees I climbed
and the way being fourteen was so sad
and scary in a family where my step-father touched me

and no one rang an alarm, not ever.
You don't want to hear,
I don't blame you.
It's ugly, glass breaking all around me,
in an old night, in a dark that is dangerous,
a shard of a family, brittle pieces of history,
casualties of war.

BERLINER ZEITUNG

Across Germany, the train tracks have healed.
Across Poland, cicatrix are closing,
        Where the woman cried out, cried out.
I made it. I lived through it.
Auchswitz grows a carpet of edelweiss, and it's real.
        That sweet smell.
The tiny faces, shaking in the wind.
In Austria, cafes re-open.
Newspapers speak the truth,
        every way we fold them.
Cafe mit schlag.
A dash of cinnamon, sharp and sweet.
The memory doesn't pierce, but soars.
The woman says no and means it.
The museums are open, and Freud's house is closed.
No one climbs on that tedious, hard couch again.
They go to see the Klimts.
Golden men and women in shimmering embrace.
See how he leans over her, he takes her up in himself as
        if she were precious.
And she finally is.
I'm standing in that gallery now.
On the boulevard, the echoes have finally died away.
Silence moves in waltz time again, the Strauss of quiet.
Everywhere rallies are over.
And Jesse Owens runs the mile in a blaze of possible.
That memory is left.
When the people cheer, it is for him, and he is winning.

Judith Rafaela

THE QUESTIONS REMAIN
For Judy Chicago's "Holocaust Project: From Darkness into Light"

The questions remain:
how to forgive god
and find praise for creation
from the ash of destruction
of our mothers, our teachers.

The question remains
what have we learned?
What changes have we wrought from our grief
forged from the fires,
blinded by the smoke and burning tears.
We wander farther and farther
into a secular wilderness,
assimilating
or from another tribe:
saying "it can't happen to us."

To face down into the pit of our past
feel…
impossible.
We spin stories of heroism or
dream dreams of what we would have done
we read fictional works
cry at movies, blame the victims,
anything,
but face our complicity and current weakness.
The past in retrospect remains so clear—
the genocides of today
vague shadows.
What are we meant to do?

We want the light without the dark,
the understanding without the pain or passion—
tidy wrapped crinkling plastic between us
and the smells of fear and death.
We have trouble naming You
great power of the universe.
We are slow to learn and slower still to forgive.

We ask the strength, therefore, to see
and remember.
To find each day the small paths of peace:
in queues and traffic.
To tear from our eyes cobwebs of denial,
to recognize our brothers and sisters
in whatever guise you present them,
to stop the genocide.

The question remains:
if we forgive You, will we take on ourselves
the burden of change,
to lead us all from darkness into light?

Joan Logghe

WHAT I'VE NOTICED ABOUT DEATH
Elegy for Bill Gersh

Is that after the breathing stops
the world starts breathing us.
Odd objects recollect us and exhale.
I can't drive north because my compass
needle is Bill Gersh, last seen as ashes.

Lilacs have already told me
all about the past. Make a shrine
of Cadillacs and soap. Collect the toll
in Yiddish. Tears for breakfast.
Pancakes in the underground garage.

My dead insect collection starts
singing about cicadas and romance,
the puta bumblebee, the fast
millipede for the end of the millennium.
Not to mention superficial mosquitoes singing scat.

Say the word death once in your outrageous voice
and my husband's sobs flew into May
like airmail straight from grief. Par Avion.
Hasta baby. Your elegy is made of chrome
and oil paint. The color wheel, a map of France.

I recommend my art to study with your breath
learning the wild pleasure of truth. Poetry,
you'd say, is something absent when the lights on.
Schmear prayers on us dumb mortals.
Tell whatever God gobbled you to spit

your spirit out whole, tangy, breathing
that God breath. Mazel to your daughters
old colossal, rain down mitzvahs, hold
the tsouris. Giving all our middle years
an alpine glow. Good sunsets from Lama Mountain

old hubcaps and white jackets. In immortality,
I hear your voice now, healthier than last week
nothing like zero for clean bill of health.
Perfecto once more. One Gorgeous Grief.
Bill Gersh, I'm tearing my clothes into Yiddish.

I want to sit shivah with a minyan of artists
and say the Kaddish all night, I'm not sleepy.
Cover the mirrors so they don't see us dancing.
You can drink anything in heaven and send me down
your holy drunkness for my new enriched art.

EVE

Eve
dead child of the desert,
Eve among women,
no one's Eve,
the night scratches and moans,
the wind rocks you, dead child
of the desert.

Eve
jewish and somber child
in this desert of strangers,
the cracked earth
sinks and calls you
Eve of the deserts,
jewish and somber child.

Your mother
Eve of the deserts,
forgot the rituals and
said that your name would be
like a supplication
in the evening wind.

In Guara
they buried you
among the high plains,
you were the only jewish child in the desert,
your mother
wrapped you
in a white coffin
with white prayers,
and white stars,
and you were a white bride

EVA

Eva
niña muerta del desierto,
Eva de las mujeres,
Eva de nadie,
la noche rasguña y gime,
el viento te mece niña muerta del
desierto.

Eva
niña judía y sola
en este desierto de extraños,
la tierra agrietada
se hunde y te llama
Eva de los desiertos,
niña judía y sola.

Tu madre
Eva de los desiertos,
olvidó los ritos y
dijo que tu nombre sería
como una plegaria
en el viento de la noche.

En Guara
entre los altiplanos
te enterraron,
eras la única niña judía en el desierto,
tu madre
te envolvió
en un ataúd blanco
con blancas plegarias,
con estrellas blancas,
y eras la novia blanca
en este oscuro sombrío desierto.

in this dark and somber desert.

Eve
jewish and somber child of the desert,
now you care
for the dead,
giving them water
and singing to them in ancient Hebrew
supplications that your mother could not invent.

Eve
dead child of the desert,
your body is a blanket of stars
a white prayer shawl.

Translated by Celeste Kostopulos-Cooperman

Eva
niña judía y sola del desierto,
ahora tú cuidas
a los muertos,
ahora les das agua
y les cantas en el Hebreo antiguo
las plegarias que tu madre no pudo inventar.

Eva
niña judía del desierto,
tu cuerpo es un manto de estrellas,
una mantilla blanca de rezos.

CONVERSOS

Like out of two fruits comes one nectar
Like the child born of father and mother
Cannot choose who he loves more
Faith is born
That our same God will mysteriously unite us
In some way, one fine day full of love

—Consuelo Luz
from ONE FINE DAY FULL OF LOVE

Robin Becker

THE CRYPTO-JEWS

This summer, reading the history of the Jews of Spain,
I learned Fra Alfonso listed "holding philosophical discussions"
as a Jewish crime. I think of the loud fights
between me and my father when he would scream that only a Jew
could love another Jew. I love the sad proud history
of expulsion and wandering, the Moorish synagogue walled
in the Venetian ghetto, persistence of study and text.
If we are the old Christ-killers on the handles of walking sticks,
we've walked the earth as calves, owls, and scorpions.
In New Mexico, the descendants of Spanish *conversos* come forth
to confess: tombstones in the yard carved with Stars of David,
no milk with meat, generations raised without pork.
What could it mean, this Hebrew script,
in grandmother's Catholic hand? Oh, New World, we drift
from eviction to eviction, go underground,
emerge in a bark on a canal, minister to kings, adapt to extreme
weather, peddle our goods and die into the future.

Beth Enson

ROSA DE CASTILLA

My friend Terésa wears a Chai
on the same gold chain as her crucifix.
Sephardic nose, a nervous intensity in her eyes,
her speech. She rolls out the dough

on the flowered oilcloth,
adds a spoonful of filling,
folds over the crust into a half-moon,
seals the edges with the tines of a fork.

Old flavors travel down the bloodlines.
The same prune and apricot jams
fill hamentashen and empanaditas.
Desert fruits, preserved with care. She tells me,

"He knew every line of the old Hebrew prayer,
said they prayed it only during storms.
My Hebrew teacher explained:
they could pray out loud and not be heard."

When she asked him,
"Grandpa, could it be
we're Jewish?" He answered,
"Why has no one asked me this before?"

Like the Rosa de Castilla
blooming copper and crimson at my door
grafted and hoarded from Moorish gardens
to courtyards of Spain's golden age

root stock transplanted
to America's red clay soil
the same blood rises to our cheeks
in hot recognition.

Isabelle Medina Sandoval

TESHUVAH

Glad tidings
Cousin Rabbi
blood of my blood of Spain.

Many years
more than forty years
my family lived in the Sinai Desert
without a temple to pray.

Many years
more than four hundred years
my family lived in the deserts of Mexico
without a temple to pray.

Cousin Rabbi
being from the anusim
what is my road to teshuvah?
I need a temple to pray.

Many years
many centuries
have been spent in the deserts
without a temple to pray.

Cousin Rabbi
we are of the same race. I need your advice.
I am dying in this eternal desert of life.

Ay, ay, ay, ay.
I do not understand my road. I need to cry.

TESHUVAH

Albricias
Primo Rabi
sangre de mi sangre de España.

Munchos años
más de cuarenta años
vivía mi familia en el desierto de Sinai
sin templo de orar.

Munchos años
más de cuatrocientos años
vivía mi familia en los desiertos de Mexico.

Primo Rabi
siendo de los anusim
¿qué es mi camino de teshuvah?
Necesito templo de orar.

Munchos años
Munchos siglos
han pasado en los desiertos
sin templo de orar.

Primo Rabi
semos de la misma raza. Necesito tus consejos.
Estoy muriendo en este desierto eterno de la vida.

Ay, ay, ay, ay.
No comprendo mi camino. Necesito llorar.

Isabelle Medina Sandoval

OPENED LOCKS

Like a foreign country filled with adventures
we played on our Grandmother's high bed
knowing that the glass door knob of the door
is a way of travelling to other new worlds.
A ray of light escapes from the lock.

The keys of the doors are in the kitchen
to hide the profound secrets of the rooms
near the cupboard that Uncle Rachel bought for us
in a house where saints do not look through walls.
Rays of light escape from the house.

We separated and twenty years passed in
different states and we united for the first time
talking about the Jewish feeling we have
in the privateness of our understanding and being.
Keys of thoughts open up our conversation.

Piles of doors of pine and heavy paints
and ports of cities and ancient places of
customs foods and families shine like
the rock of the menorah on our Grandma's land.
Fires of light and keys illuminate our souls.

The Sephardim of Spain escaped with a hidden key
and I know deep in my bones that this same key was lost
and that now we have found the key to the sleeping neshama.

TRANCAS ABIERTAS

Como un país extraño lleno de aventuras
jugamos en la camalta de nuestra abuelita
sabiendo que la bola de vidrio de la puerta
es manera de viajar a otros mundos nuevos.
Un rayito de luz escapa de la tranca.

Las llaves de las puertas están en la cocina
para esconder secretos profundos de los cuartos
cerca del trastero que nos compró tío Raquel
en una casa donde santos no miran por paredes.
Rayitos de luz escapan de la casita.

Nos separamos y veinte años pasaron en
estados diferentes y juntamos y por la primera
vez hablando del sentido judío que tenemos
en el privado de nuestro entendimiento y ser.
Llaves de pensamientos abren nuestra plática.

Pilas de puertas de pino y pintas pesadas
y puertos de ciudades y lugares ancianos de
costumbres comidas y familias brillan como
la piedra con la menora del terreno de la abuelita.
Lumbres de luz y llaves iluminan nuestros almas.

Los sefarditos de España se escaparon con llave escondida
y sé dentro de mis huesos que esta misma llave fue perdida
y que ya hemos encontrado la llave en la neshama dormida.

Isabelle Medina Sandoval

A MOTHER'S PRAYER

Señor Most High
Father of my life
here in the mountains
of New Mexico
I ask you for blessings
for my children.
Señor I belong to you.
Señor I belong to you.

God of Abraham
God of Isaac
God of Jacob
God of this mother
God of Israel
God of this world.
Señor I belong to you.
Señor I belong to you.

That my children
and their children
will have a good life.
My children belong to you
and our dreams belong to you.
Señor I belong to you.
Señor I belong to you.

Praise be the Eternal.
Do not forget us
so far from our family
so far from my Padre.
Señor I belong to you.
Señor I belong to you.

Isabelle Medina Sandoval

ORACIÓN DE UNA MADRE

Señor Altísimo
Padre de mi vida
aquí en las montañas
de Nuévo Mexico
te pido bendiciones
para mis hijos.
Señor yo soy tuya.
Señor yo soy tuya.

Dios de Abraham
Dios de Ysaque
Dios de Jacob
Dios de esta madre
Dios de Ysrael
Dios del mundo.
Señor yo soy tuya.
Señor yo soy tuya.

Que mis hijos
y sus hijos
tengan buena vida.
Mis hijos son tuyos
y nuestros sueños son tuyos.
Señor yo soy tuya.
Señor yo soy tuya.

Alabado es el Eterno.
No te nos olvides
tan lejos de familia
tan lejos de mi Padre.
Señor yo soy tuya.
Señor yo soy tuya.

Long live our King
Long live our Law
Long live Adonai.
Señor I belong to you.
Señor I belong to you.
Señor my children belong to you.
Señor my children belong to you.
Señor I belong to you.
Señor I belong to you.

Long live our King
Long live our King.
Long live our Law
Long live our Law.
Long live Adonai
Long live Adonai.

Viva Nuestro Rey
Viva Nuestra Ley
Viva Adonai.
Señor yo soy tuya.
Señor yo soy tuya.
Señor mis hijos son tuyos.
Señor mis hijos son tuyos.
Señor yo soy tuya.
Señor yo soy tuya.

Viva Nuestro Rey
Viva Nuestro Rey.
Viva Nuestra Ley
Viva Nuestra Ley.
Viva Adonai
Viva Adonai.

Elmo Mondragón

AFTER THE INQUISITION

The stars at night read like an ancient text
it's writing shattered and spilled out against the sky.
At night the sea comforts.
Its immensity masked
it lulls and beats against the ship
murmuring like a lullaby.
We have brought nothing with us
faced with a certain death we chose a certain death.
We have delivered ourselves from the hands of our tormentors
into the less bloody hands of their brothers.
Father, my every breath is filled with *no more.*
No more to hear the startled cries
the distant sound of horses' hooves
then suddenly the frenzied crowd.
No more to see the withered arms
or horrid scars conversion brings.
I'd rather we be devoured
by the wolves of the new world
than face the searing iron
bringing tranformation to the soul.
Already Maria's body swells
and we have still to reach those shores.
But this new life will find the sustenance
of sunlight and earth and rain and snow.
And like her father the marrow of her bones
will cry out, constantly cry out: *no more.*

Isabelle Medina Sandoval

SONGBIRD OF THE SEFARAD

Nesting in the safe *colonia* of her birth
the parents loved the curly-haired *criatura*
and nourished her with warmth.
Then the songbird of the Sefarad
cantaba in the tree of life...

Que lindo es el mundo.
How beautiful is the world.
Sitting in the poor minority school
teachers shunned the brown female
and deprived her of growth.

Todo es feo. Si yo tuviera el cabello rubio.
Everything is ugly. If only I had blond hair.
Drifting along she searched
for her own kind and found no one.

Me siento tan solita. No encuentro al Eterno en la iglesia.
I feel so alone. I do not find G-d in church.
Floating like a lost duckling
she knew she did not belong.

And the songbird of the Sefarad *cantaba* in the tree of life...
Hay más en este mundo. Vuelo yo tan solita.
There is more in this world. I fly so alone.
Resting in the early afternoon
feelings of being different
inundated her being in her *colorado* clay form.
And the songbird of the Sefarad *cantaba* in the tree of life...

¿Quien soy yo? ¿Por qué soy tan diferente?
Who am I ? Why am I so different?

Perching on the gateway of *La Ceja del Norte* the migrating
flock of birds hovered in a mystical pine consumed in the
realization that her natal self-disclosure was imminent.
As the regal songbird of the Sefarad *cantaba* in the tree of life...

La canción de la Sefarad es para ti.
The song of the Sefarad is for you.

Revealing themselves to her in the branches in shimmering
hues of metallic wings with purple breasts and ruby faces
and crowned with a blue star on the forehead they warbled
Hija mía, listen to your heart. Heed the message and
you will fly on the eternal wings of the splendid Sefarad.

Strumming the breathing pine boughs of the spiritual tree
the wind orchestrated haunting Spanish strings resonating
celestial harmony as the songbirds trill in undiluted concert.
While the wise songbird of the Sefrad sings...
Like a bird in migration your instincts guide you.

Do you remember hearing Ladino music for the first time?
I, the Songbird of the Sefarad, understood the impact of
the inherent relevance permeating each fiber of your
being as the cabbalistic realization overpowers you.
Human rationalization cannot comprehend. You know my
voice. Those who hear my music are part of the flock.

Like the ugly duckling transformed to the exotic rare bird,
your cryptic imprinting binds you to us for eternity.
Drink of my nectar and you will grow. You belong to
the Sefarad. You are strong. Your blue star is your compass.

Lifting her camouflaged wings in arched symmetry
the royal bird found her flock and flapped her feeble
wings and began to glide with her species on their journey.

And the songbirds of the Sefarad sang:
My daughter. Welcome home. *Oye O Ysrael*
*Tú eres el mismo siempre y tus días no tendrán fin.**
Praised be Adonay. Baruch Adonay Baruch.

*You are the same always and your days have no end. (Psalm 102)

Isabelle Medina Sandoval

MAMACITA MI HERMANA

Tender like the doncella of the Mora mist
the gentle israelita tended the sheep and
guarded and played with the goats in high
mountain vegas as did her people before
her in Eretz Israel and in the Sefarad.

Soft like the creation the swirling clouds
of her amniotic fluids nourished me as
her maternal mikve bequeathed the perpetual
Jewish legacy in my own genetic form coding
and extending me to multigenerational mishpaha.

Caring like the watchful thundercloud vapor
making me memorize the Ten Commandments
reminding me of my physical Jewish appearance
cautioning me not to go down to Egypt and final
words instructing me to worship only on the Sabbath.

Living like the quixotic and cabalistic sangre
flowing in my veins foggy memories of an ancient
Sara prenada and sefardita mothers whispering
and uncovering my antiquated veils crescendo in
many paridas celebrating their long awaited birth.

Mamacita mi mana
tu eres mi hermana
semos hijas de Sara.

Isabelle Medina Sandoval

CONTEMPORARY INQUISITION

EDICT OF GRACE
Propelled by the drive of the impetus
of Spain's exploration to the New World
I stand in the Portal of Secrecy in the Americas.

RESPONSA
My family and I plead guilty to the following offenses…
Observing the Sabbath and preparing food on Friday
Drinking kosher wine and not making the sign of the cross
Burning fingernails and cutting the throats of fowls like the Jews
Lighting Friday candles and throwing bits of *masa* into the fire
Washing off the sacrament of baptism of the children and
Eating *pan de semita* during *La Semana Santa.*

In the name of G-d, I plead guilty.

TRIAL

Family—How dare you tell our family secrets and
destroy our image in the community and in the church?

Reporters—Tell me your story and I will construct my theory
of Crypto Jews and I may even give you a copy of my work.

Religious Leaders—Who is your mother? And your father?
We need to document them in our international data base.

Spanish Colonists—*Y, que cosa*, the Jews killed the Christ.
We came in the name of Spain and in the Holy Catholic Church.

General Population —Is it possible that some of the first
Spanish colonists were really Sephardic Jews?

Anusim Friends—Do not reveal too much. We know who
we are and they will only hurt us and expose us to others.

Researchers—Yes, some Sephardic Jews did travel with
Juan Pérez de Oñate to settle New Mexico in 1598.

Jews—What a very interesting topic for further study.
I see the connection of Crypto Jews in the Southwest.

Tía—We know we are Jews, *mi hija*. It is just that we
have been *católicos por muncho y muncho tiempo*.

Chicano—Hijola. You embarass me *muncho*. You deny your
Indian *sangre*. You are a *mestizo* just like me.

Historians—Prove that you are Jewish. We need facts.
Hispanos did not read or write. We need to study your proof.

Collective Memory—You know deep inside you are a Jew.
How do you balance the legecy of your ancient mishpaha?

CASA DE LA PENITENCIA

While in my five hundred year mud prison mortal
resting in the diffusing sunlight of the shady portal
figures pass speaking of Maimonides and Aristotle.

SACO BENDITO

I am dressed in the habit of the yellow robe and the
black cross surrounded by the dove of Protestantism
and guarded by the *suerte* of my *Estrella de David*.
I feel deep *vergüenza* for the shame on my family.

AUTO DE FE

Religious Leader—Your family is stained with heretical Jewish
practices. Come with us and I will give you absolution. Why
would you choose to be persecuted as a woman Hispanic and now a
Jewess? Who knows what time may bring? Come my
daughter and I will give your peace and protection. What will
your employer and loved ones say? Have you thought of future
historical implications for your children and unborn babes?

Orthodox Rabbi —I have compassion for Crypto Jews. Vestiges
of customs and Jewish practices are evident. However you must
prove an unbroken matrilineal descent or undergo halakhic
conversion. You must convert to prove your true faith.

Liberal Rabbi—I have listened to your story and have studied
your case. If you feel in your heart that you descend from a
Jewish line you do not need to go through conversion. You
must know that you will not have any standing in Eretz Ysrael.

CASA DE LA PENITENCIA

Contemplating the safety of the adobe earth
I long to step outside the portal and begin my birth
and end my soul's five centuries of dismal dreaded dearth.

And inside my adamic glass ceiling bottle
electronic hummings of Don Isaac parade a coffle
lighting the *Camino Real* as I follow my gate's marrano throttle.

Notes from the Office of the Inquisition

Like melodic Spanish castanets dancing with the AT&T baron
this anusim force shepherds the gateway to the Rose of Sharon.

Quemadero de Computadora

My marrano portal cries out
for spiritual guidance on this Sephardic route.
Will someone help me dismantle these human doubts?

A.S. Gintzler

POR SOSPECHOSO JUDÍO

Francisco Gómez Robledo,
        b. 1628 in Santa Fe,
        Sargento Mayor of the local militia,
had a brother who had a *colita*—
(witnesses saw it when he was swimming)—
a small Jewish tail.

Por sospechoso judío —a trial,
For suspicion of being a Jew—
marrano, a swine, demon defile.

En Nuevo Méjico y en Tejas,
Luis the Younger defied Inquisition,
On banks of the *Río Panuco*,
Circumcised himself, like Abraham,
while I held the tip in position,
kin, while he severed his foreskin.

And in his Inquisition cell,
Luis nurtured his soul,
and starved his body
to fit through the bars,
to preach Judaism to other swine,
meditation and prayer
to his grandmother's god.

A crime it was
to Judaize —*por judaizante*
But crime no more,
Pero no hay, there are no
Jewish symbols on my New Mexican door.

Secret-Jew am I,
Remembering
Spaniards burned at the stake,
in *autos-de-fe* of saintly faith,
still present, *presente.*

Don Bernardo López (*marrano*),
   Governor of New Mexico (1659-1661), *Presente!*
Juan Gómez Barragan (*marrano*),
   soldier-escort in New Mexico, *Presente!*
Luis de Carvajal (*marrano*),
   first Spanish Governor north of Mexico, *Presente!*
Doña Francisca Carvajal, and her daughters,
Isabel, Catalina, Leonor, *y* Mariana,
marranas burned alive at the stake,
in Mexico City, a holy occasion.

But when the Fires of Faith rose,
before the Cathedral *en la Plaza Grande,*
Holy winds tore down Pharisee tents,
and whipped the crowd to fear.

Four centuries later, we circumcised my son, in Santa Fe,
City of Holy Faith, according to the Law of Moses,
(we left his *colita,* though).

Joan Logghe

SOMETHING

Sophía had a secret even Sophía
didn't know. Something about
candles at night, no taste of pork
in her grandmother's house. Something.

Shadowed memory of her grandmother
in her dark bedroom, her voice nearly
a whisper, "It passes down through the women."
That and "Tell your daughter."

Something about the farolitos lined up,
a top to spin. "Our family came from Spain,
not Mexico, hundreds of years ago, you know.
This is your great-grandfather, Israel.

See how handsome he was." Sophía recalls it all,
but mixed with other recollections, the smell
of pine at Christmas, candles at mass,
the sight of blood at butchering each fall.

Something about candles to Saint Esther.
It didn't make sense. "We came here from Spain.
Look hard at this photograph." Her mother's voice
in the kitchen light, flour in the air.

She'd tell her daughters something soon.
She's been meaning to. For hundreds of years.
She'll tell them soon. She will.

Consuelo Luz

ONE FINE DAY FULL OF LOVE

Encendiendo velas a escondidas
Bebés varones lloran en sagrado dolor
Qué será esto, di, Padre di
La amarga eternidad de
  esconderse así
De cortinas cerradas y antiguas
  canciones
De voces calladas y amortiguadas
  pasiones
Por la gracia de un sagrado misterio
En dos mundos sabemos vivir

Lighting candles in hiding
Baby boys cry in holy pain
What is this, say, Father, say
The bitter eternity of hiding in
  this way
Of closed curtains and ancient
  songs
Of hushed voices and muffled
  passions
By the grace of a great sacred mystery
In two worlds we have learnt how
to live

Two lives, two loves, Sabbath candles light up Good Friday
Two hearts in one, La Virgen sees it all
We never thought we'd learn to love so deeply
Our Santos all and that man upon the cross

Two lives, two loves living in just one body
Two hearts in one, a Soul that's split in two
Such is the fate of one who prays in secret
And yet one day that Soul will sing as One

Como el hombre que ama a dos mujeres
Como el pájaro que le gusta nadar
Como cuando al mismo tiempo
  sale el sol y llueve
Como de dos frutas sale un manjar

Like the man who loves two women
Like the bird who loves to swim
Like when the sun comes out in
  the rain
Like out of two fruits comes one
  nectar

Como el niño que nace de un
    padre y una madre
No puede escoger al quien ama
    más
Nace la fe
    en el misterio
Que Dios nos unirá
    en un día lleno de amar

Like the child born of father
    and mother
Cannot choose who he loves
    more
Faith is born
    that our same God will
    mysteriously unite us
In some way, one fine day, full of
    love

BIOGRAPHIES AND ACKNOWLEGEMENTS

MARJORIE AGOSÍN

Marjorie Agosín is Professor of Spanish at Wellesley College and a poet, writer, critic, and an untiring human rights activist. She is the descendant of European Jews who fled the Holocaust and settled in Chile. She has been in exile from Chile since 1972. She is the author of *A Cross and a Star: Memoirs of a Jewish Girl in Chile* (The University of New Mexico Press), 18 books of poetry, fiction, and short stories. In 1990 she received the Jeanneta Rankin Award for Achievement in Human Rights. In 1995 she received the Letras de Oro Award for *Noche Estrallada* and the Latino Literature Prize for *Hacia la Ciudad Espléndida*.

ROBIN BECKER

Robin Becker Writes: "References to secular American Judaism began appearing in my poems in the 1970's. In 1982, I wrote: "The road to Chimayo / winds / up the mountain / & down / to the fleshy foothills. / They open, pink, like the folds / of skin— / clean, loose, soft— / on my grandmother's / upper arm & belly." With this poem, "Old Women and Hills," I made an explicit connection between the familial "body" and New Mexico geography. On the high desert, in Taos, I feel close to the ancestral desert of my imagination and to Israel. The insider / outsider tension I feel as a Jewish lesbian feminist in mainstream North America is made even more vivid in the clarifying light of Taos mesa. I teach poetry writing and book reviewing at Penn State Universtiy. *All-American Girl* (University of Pittsburgh Press) won the 1996 Lambda Literary Award in Lesbian Poetry."

"The Crypto-Jews" and "Yom Kippur, Taos, New Mexico" are from *All-American Girl*, by Robin Becker, copyright 1996. Reprinted by permission of the University of Pittsburgh Press.

BETH ENSON

"In Taos, NM, I am an editor with Blinking Yellow Books, a small press. I also volunteer with the Society of the Muse of the Southwest (S.O.M.O.S.).

"I feel a strong affinity for my roots in Eastern European poetry and literature, particularly the Russians and Poles. The Yiddish writers—Singer, Babel, Aleichem—have also shown the way with their concern for the small, mundane, funny aspects of life and spirit.

"Coming to New Mexico and joining a family with four centuries of roots in the land here has thrown into relief my sense of being Jewish as wanderer, borderbreaker, outsider, and cross-pollinator. I love this land but will never belong to it in the same way my daughter (due to be born any day now) will. My homeland is in books, language, and poetry. This begins to feel as solid and nourishing as earth the more I read and write."

MAX FINSTEIN

Max Finstein said in his work: "I'm a glorylickin' fightin' knight in hopeless armor." Max was a well-loved Taos poet. Among his publications were *Disappearance of Mountains* (Wild Dog Press), *There Is Always a Moon in America* (Cranium Press), and *Savonarola's Tune and Selected Poems* (Desert Review Press).

Each year at the Taos Poetry Circus, the Finstein Memorial Trophy, nicknamed "the Max," is given to the World Heavyweight Championship Poetry Bout winner.

YEHUDIS FISHMAN

"Writing poetry has been a closet interest since I was three. Being a teacher and a lecturer on Judaism has been a front door occupation for over thirty years. During my eight years of living in Santa Fe, since leaving the east coast, the front door has somewhat receded while the closet door has opened. I came here to do a little teaching, and to work on a book about women and the Bible. In the secret spaces, I found my dormant interest in poetry slipping out, perhaps partially due to the beauty of the land and the gaps between independent Jewish souls planted sparingly between the sometimes congestive conformity of Jewish coastal communities. Though feelings of isolation creep up occasionally, thanks to the wonder of computers, I can keep in touch with friends back east, and still find time—again with the help of my computer—to dabble with the magical ingredients of combining the ambience of the Southwest with my consuming love of Judaism."

GENE FRUMKIN

"My Jewish background is always lurking in the wings. I am a secular Jew, but was raised in an Orthodox household (Latvian-Lithuanian) whose roots remain underground in two senses: alive but sometimes hidden.

"It was a real adventure for me coming to New Mexico in 1966 from Los Angeles where I had spent 28 years. Also being born in New York City, I felt an added strangeness in my new city, which of course was very much smaller than what I had been used to. Albuquerque felt to me then as an overgrown cow town. I relished it—especially as a Jew—it was almost as if I were walking around as a Jewish cowboy or Indian, no matter which.

"New Mexico as a whole gave my Jewishness a good airing out, a sense of nature that I'd never experienced before. Once, driving from the city to Placitas, NM, some 20 miles away, I had to pull over and stop my car just to look at the stars. This was during my first two months in New Mexico, and I haven't stopped looking since."

His most recent collection of poems is *The Old Man Who Swam Away and Left Only His Wet Feet* (La Alameda Press). "The Singer of Manoa Street" appeared in his previous book *Saturn Is Mostly Weather: Selected and Uncollected Poems* (Cinco Puntos Press).

BILL GERSH

Bill Gersh was an artist and sculptor whose work focused on found object assemblage and collage, drawing that incorporated primitive iconography, and painting encompassing his investigation of Mayan culture, Greek mythology and Tantric imagery. His work, sometimes classified as outlaw modernist or abstract expressionist, is in many private collections throughout the country, as well as museum collections in the state.

Writing was as natural an expression of his effusive creativity as his visual explorations. Gersh, though quintessentially Jewish, did not often write or paint directly from Jewish themes. Rather, he lived them—as a charmingly obsessive sweeper of floors, window cleaner, over protective mother, guilt-ridden father. In his art he was always reaching out to other cultures who share the periphery.

A. S. GINTZLER

Brooklyn-born and raised, A. S. Gintzler has worked as writer and editor for magazines, book publishers, and network television. He authored the six-book *Rough & Ready* series on the Old West, the forthcoming novel *Angel In My Pocket,* and *The Call,* a screenplay.

"My earliest unself-conscious writing, as I remember it, drew on nightmare and an obscure grasping after God. Strands of American pluralism, *Yiddishkeit,* blue-collar-folk-intellectuality, and mystical striving braid my writing today. Tribal and cultural taproots run deep in New Mexico—history and time compressed in a vertical, transcendent present—familiar and fertile ground for a son of Jacob."

JENNY GOLDBERG

Jenny Goldberg lives north of Taos, NM. Of "Song of Wildfire" she writes: "After the 1996 Hondo Fire burned my friends' house on Lama Mountain where we had begun to build a community, we had a ceremonial circle. As we held hands and prayed, I gazed at the surrounding houses all untouched by the fire, at the emaciated, charred trees calling forth the holocaust, at the little green shoots coming up through ashes. I felt chosen, purified, in love with life. The rich heritage in Northern New Mexico inspires me to look at my own Jewish roots—endurance, resilience, exile, and rededication to the bonds of God and life."

NATALIE GOLDBERG

"Robert Creeley called New Mexico the 'Goyim's Israel.' I'm an American Jew. Somewhere in my roots I long for desert and have found it here among chamisa, sage, Russian olive.

A long time ago, I went to my Zen teacher and told him: 'The more I meditate, the more Jewish I feel.'

'That makes sense,' he responded. 'The more you sit, the more you become who you are.'

The more I write, the more my writing comes from a Jewish heart, from Jewish hands and from a Jewish mouth full of Jewish love."

Natalie Goldberg is the author of *Writing Down the Bones*, *Wild Mind*, *Long Quiet Highway*, *Banana Rose*, and *Living Color*. She lives on a mesa in Taos, NM.

RABBI LYNN GOTTLIEB

Rabbi Lynn Gottlieb is Rabbi of Nahalat Shalom an independent, Jewish renewal congregation in Albuquerque, NM. She is noted for storytelling and midrash and is the author of *She Who Dwells Within: A Feminist Vision of a Renewed Judiasm*.

"Mother Chant" is from *She Who Dwells Within* by Lynn Gottlieb, copyright 1995 Lynn Gottlieb, reprinted by permission of HarperCollins Publishers, Inc.

JUDYTH HILL

Judyth Hill is a writer, performer, and teacher of poetry, living where the Rockies meet the Plains, near Las Vegas, NM. She is the director of Literary Projects for New Mexico Arts, a Division of the Office of Cultural Affairs.

She has authored five books of poetry including, *A Presence of Angels* (Sherman Asher Publishing) and *Men Need Space* (Sherman Asher Publishing). Her work is included in numerous anthologies. Her newest title, a cookbook with poetry and essays, *The Dharma of Baking: Recipes from Chocolate Maven*, is forthcoming from Ten Speed Press in Berkeley, CA. She was described by the St. Helena Examiner as "energy with skin".

Born Jewish, raised Reform, she began to study Judaism seriously with "The Minyan", Santa Fe's first Reconstructionist congregation. Judyth says: "Being Jewish is part of me like the color of my eyes, or my sense of humor. Rather than a focus, it's a lens, a sensibility that suffuses my connections with this miraculous, sacred, ordinary world we are blessed to inhabit. Living in New Mexico is exactly like being Jewish: A State of Grace."

"Grapes from the Fishman", "Berliner Zeitung", "Listen Carefully", and "Star Children" are from *Hardwired for Love* (Pennywhistle Press). "Advice From Nana" appeared in *Bubbe Meisehs: Poetry by Jewish Granddaughters* (HerBooks). "Angels and Thorns" is from *A Presence of Angels* (Sherman Asher Publishing). "Mrs. Noah" will appear in the forthcoming Israeli anthology *Details Omitted from the Text.*

PHYLLIS HOTCH

"New Mexico's landscape and lifestyle present a dramatic contrast to my early years in the Bronx—Jewish and Italian neighbors, taking the streetcars and elevated trains to school—and later suburban Massachusetts. But Taos mountains, sky, and mesa claimed me and

I responded with loving gratitude. Perhaps it is an ancient similarity of place, before New York or the Eastern Europe of great grandparents, that makes it home."

Her work has appeared in many journals and anthologies including *The Threepenny Review*, *The Woman's Review of Books*, *XY Files: Poems on the Male Experience* (Sherman Asher Publishing), and *The Practice of Peace* (Sherman Asher Publishing). Her most recent title is *A Little Book of Lies* (Blinking Yellow Books).

SHULI LAMDEN

"My poems have appeared in the *California Quarterly*, *Poets On*, *Blue Mesa Review*, and *New Frontiers Magazine*. I teach basic reading, writing, and study skills at Santa Fe Community College. Both my teaching and writing are my Jewish identity. When I moved to New Mexico in 1983, I was struck by the similarities between this landscape and my images of Israel. One great day that year, my car got stuck in mud on an isolated dirt road north of Abiquiu. To get home, my friend and I had to wait all day until the road froze up. We had no food with us, but we did have our grad school reading assignment for the next day: the book of Exodus. There in the desert, we savored that nourishment, and God delivered us to US 84 at about one in the morning."

JOAN LOGGHE

"When I moved to New Mexico in 1973 I did not advertise the fact that I was Jewish. Then I started writing again in 1980 and became more and more Jewish, as I became more revealed to myself. When the news of the crypto-Jews broke, I got chills. I felt I had always been a bit hidden. I am out now. As a writer I've published books, written reviews, and won an NEA grant in poetry and a Barbara Deming Grant for translation of the Sofía poems into Spanish. New Mexico has held me for this life, as has my Jewish upbringing."

"Something" is from *What Makes a Woman Beautiful* (Pennywhistle Press), "Always Aunt Clara" first appeared in the 1995 Temple Beth Shalom's *Calendar of Jewish Artists.*

CONSUELO LUZ

Consuelo Luz lives in Santa Fe, NM, and hosts a national daily Spanish radio program called *Buscando la Belleza / In Search of Beauty*. She has published and translated poetry in *¡Saludos!* (Pennywhistle Press) and will soon release her third musical recording, *Neshama*, in which she sings contemporized versions of ancient Sephardic songs in Hebrew and Ladino.

"It is my birthday, October 8, 1981. My future husband takes me down from our mountain village isolation to Santa Fe to my first Yom Kippur. In infancy perhaps I had a birthday so drenched in spirit. This day of weeping at the Gates of Repentance is a different kind of confession than the Catholic one I grew up with, it is confession multiplied like a million stones gathering, gathering into a riverbed of memory and mercy, a year's worth of confessions, a year's worth of grace. That's a lot of grace. I swim in it. The wrenching river of compassion, prayers, music takes me to the doors of the Gate and beyond, back through time, ancient roots and into a present of soul searching in the exquisite poetry of stark, beautiful words that sear my heart and open it to the depths of who I am and why I am here, strip me down to the humility of being 'a whisper lost among the stars...a moment in the flow of time', yes, only a moment but 'an eternal moment in God's hands'.

"I face myself alone but in community. I drink wisdom, eat forgiveness.

"Day of awe, day of God 'enduring as the everlasting hills', day of healing, day of commitment to live responsibly, day of letting go, day of renewing faith in Earth, in humanity, day of renewing faith in faith, of taking on Life once again, happy happy birthday praising, thanking for another chance to 'live as if all life depended on you'. YES! Inscribe me for blessing in the Book of Life!

The gates open, the sun sets on the Sangre de Cristo Mountains, the gates close, mercy flows, grace delivers.

"It is the following year, there is an ancient Torah from Romania leaning against our rough adobe wall, its faded parchment dancing in the light of our wood stove. Rescued from the Holocaust, it has arrived to serve our Taos Havurah. The Trampas River sings outside the window, beneath the Sangre de Cristos cool and breathing in the moonlight. Soft and harsh. Old and now. Eternal continuity in the face of the harshest of destinies, the Torah, surviving, traveling, flying like the Jews to faraway places to escape, to hide, to live again and again...and now again in the mountains of New Mexico.

"It is October, 1995. In my son's glowing, singing face I see the spirit of my Jewish ancestors from Avila. They are smiling in approval. My heart wets my eyes as my son Max Gabriel Paz Isidro Moishe Eliahu becomes a Bar Mitzvah. As he sings in Spanish a special song his Catholic-raised mother has written for him I give thanks for this amazing opportunity for joy, for a timeless sense of connection, of tradition, for the pride, the accomplishment, the celebration, the community. My son carries the Torah like Jesus of Nazareth did long ago. There is love all around."

MATT MEYERS

"I live alone in the Black Range Mountains of southern New Mexico, so my experience of Judaism, since moving here four years ago, has essentially been contemplative. I study Kabbalah, astrology, and have a keen interest in Zionist history. I also practice Vipassana Meditation in the tradition of S. N. Goenka of India, and Mindfulness Meditation as taught by Thich Nhat Hanh, of Plum Village, France. I currently teach Mindfulness Meditation in Truth or Consequences, NM."

"Kitchen Table" and "Snowed-In" are from his latest title, *Sacred Journey*.

CAROL MOLDAW

Carol Moldaw grew up in the San Francisco Bay Area. A recipient of an NEA Literary Fellowship in 1994, Moldaw is the author of *Chalkmarks on Stone* (La Alameda Press) and *Taken from the River* (Alef Books). She is also co-editor of a special feature of *Frank* (Paris) on New Mexican Writers. After living in Manhattan for four years, Moldaw settled in New Mexico in 1990. She lives in Pojoaque, 20 miles north of Santa Fe.

"Since moving to New Mexico, my awareness as a Jew has deepened. Judaism—its view of God, traditions, ethics, stories, and my relationship to it—is an essential and recurrent component of my work."

"Lines Begun on Yom Kippur" is in *Chalkmarks on Stone* (La Alameda Press). "Patrilineage" first appeared in *Pinchpenny* Vol. 6, No. 1 (1985), and is included in *Taken from the River* (Alef Books). "Reb Shmerl and The Water Spirit" first appeared in *The Kenyon Review (New Series)* Vol. XIV, No. 1, Winter 1992. It is also included in *Taken from the River.*

ELMO MONDRAGÓN

"This poem, 'After the Inquisition', has its inception in listening to late night television. I heard someone explain that his grandfather and grandmother both had been brought to Australia in chains, and here was his beginning. Why else, he asked, would someone go to a place so unknown and frightening? I remembered families I had known in Taos who lighted candles at Christmas, but secretly, and could not remember why. Then I thought of my own first exposure to Andalucia and the emotion it stirred in me when I saw those hills that looked so much like Taos. I remembered the communities in Southern Spain which had once been part of that time and place where Maimonides lived and thrived, and where walking those streets I felt oddly at home.

"'After the Inquisition' is a statement of my conviction, both emotional and otherwise, that here was my beginning, that my family came to New Mexico as part of a wave of migration caused by the Inquisition. In that sense it is an ancestor song and a reclaiming of the past. The poem has not been published elsewhere, and has been rarely read or shared."

JEAN NORDHAUS

Born in Baltimore, MD, and married to a native New Mexican, Jean Nordhaus lives in Washington, DC, but sojourns frequently in New Mexico. Her books of poetry include *A Bracelet of Lies* (Washington Writers' Publishing House) and *My Life in Hiding* (Quarterly Review of Literature, Vol. XXX, 1991). Her poem in this volume had its inception in family stories about her husband's great-grandmother, a nineteenth-century German-Jewish transplant to New Mexico who also appears as "The German Bride" in Paul Horgan's *Centuries of Santa Fe*.

"Santa Fe: A Jewish Wife" was originally published in *Phoebe*, Vol XVII, No. 1, Fall, 1987 and was reprinted in the *Quarterly Review of Literature 50th Anniversary Anthology* .

JUDITH RAFAELA

Judith Rafaela is currently a publisher, poet, author of *Poems Along the Path*, and editor of three anthologies *Written with a Spoon, A Poet's Cookbook; XY Files: Poems on the Male Experience*, and *The Practice of Peace* (all titles from Sherman Asher Publishing). As Judith Asher she founded Sherman Asher Publishing in 1994, a press that is committed to changing the world one book at a time by shattering stereotypes, commitment to craft, thoughtful design of books, and bringing regional voices to a wider audience. These works can be sampled at www.shermanasher.com. Judith moved to Santa Fe, NM, in the mid 70s where she practiced medicine and raised her children until, overwhelmed by the Land of Enchantment, she gave up medicine to pursue the wonder of words. She is a passionate Jew and has served at Temple Beth Shalom in Santa Fe as president, treasurer, Cantorial soloist and teacher. Nationally she has been a member of the board of Union of American Hebrew Congregations, the North American Board of the World Union for Progressive Judaism, and would like to be involved in Intergalactic Judaism. She also serves on several national organizations supporting education, art, and disability communities. These activities bring fulfillment to a lifelong love of music, performance, and stories.

"Wandering Jew" and "Atonement Songs" are from *Poems Along the Path* (Sherman Asher Publishing).

Josh Rappaport

Josh Rappaport has explored his Jewish roots in New Mexico and around the world. The fruit of his research was a radio play, "Threads," which aired on New Mexico Public Radio in 1994. Since then, Josh has applied his literary talents in a more unusual setting. A professional tutor for the past eight years, Josh recently authored the *Algebra Survival Kit* (Singing Turtle Press, 1998), a conversational guide for the thoroughly befuddled.

Barbara Rockman

"My poems circle and explore my fear of faith and my continuous struggle to find my place in an often faithless world. Though a universal struggle, mine is compounded by my irrevocable but confused identity as a Jew. It has only been in recent years that I have found comfort and inspiration in religious Jewish community. Though I tread warily toward organized religion my heart opens to the teachings of Torah, to rituals and celebrations which provide a deepfelt sense of home. As my poems are rooted in family so my new Jewishness is interwoven with my husband's steady acceptance of his faith, my young daughter's curiosity about God, and my older daughter's recent year of Torah study, questioning, and Bat Mitzvah. New Mexico's openness of land and spirit, distant from the New England propriety in which I was raised, has surely afforded literal and figurative room for my fledgling religious exploration."

She received the 1997 Recursos Discovery Award, and her MFA in Writing at Vermont College in 1998. Her poems have appeared in *Written With A Spoon: A Poet's Cookbook* (Sherman Asher Publishing) and the magazine *Are We There Yet?*

MIRIAM SAGAN

Miriam Sagan is the author of more than a dozen books, including *Tracing Our Jewish Roots* (John Muir Publications), *The Art of Love: New & Selected Poems* (La Alameda Press), *New Mexico Poetry Renaissance* co-edited with Sharon Niederman (Red Crane), and *Dirty Laundry: 100 Days in a Zen Monastery* (La Alameda Press) written with her late husband Robert Winson.

"When I came to New Mexico in 1984, the desert merged in my imagination with the wilderness of the Old Testament. Though paradoxically farther away from my New York/Russian Jewish roots, in New Mexico I rediscovered Judaism. It was here that I learned to pronounce the Hebrew alphabet, celebrated the holidays, and became a member of a synagogue. In contradiction to my socialist/atheist—though Jewish!—upbringing I found a source of spirituality among the diverse Jews of New Mexico."

"The God of the Jews" first appeared in *True Body* (Parallax Press). "Wailing Wall" and "Passover" are from *Art of Love* (La Alameda Press). "Hannuka Haiku" appeared in *Frogpond Magazine.* "Mikvah Psalm" appeared in the 1995 Temple Beth Shalom's *Calendar of Jewish Artists.*

ISABELLE MEDINA SANDOVAL

"I am an educator by profession and possess a heart and soul that mirrors the Sephardic experience of the medieval Iberian Peninsula. Researching genealogy for the past twenty years, I discovered that I descend from the original Spanish settlers who accompanied Oñate to New Mexico in 1598. My family is rooted in the beautiful

Mora Valley and I have uncovered our rich and intricate hidden Jewish past. Enduring five hundred years of forced conversion, my family demonstrates the strength of the *anousi neshama* shining in the enchanting sunsets of the Rocky Mountains. Despite the phenomenal discrimination suffered by my people, I survived and I welcome the new sunrise with alacrity in being a contemporary *anousi.*"

Isabelle serves on the board for the Hispano Crypto Jewish Resource Center in Denver, CO. She is a member of National Association of Sephardic Artists, Writers, and Intellectuals.

Her poetry has been published in *Ha Lapid, Aurora, Sephardic House, JUF News.* Her article "Abraham's Children of the Southwest" was published in the *1996 Jewish Folklore and Ethnology Review.*

"Teshuvah" appeared in *Sephardic House, Aurora, Ha Lapid,* and *Peseifas.* "Trancas Abiertas" appeared in *Llave Exhibit* of Albany, New York Sage College. "Songbird of the Sefarad" appeared in *JUF News.* "Contemporary Inquisition" appeared in *The New Mexico Jewish Link.* "Oración de una Madre" appeared in the *Colorado Springs Gazette.*

ÁNNAH SOBELMAN

"To be Jewish for me is to continually meet chords, layers of mysteries whose textures, smells, sensations are enhanced, I think by my lack of historical physical details about my father's family's past. I think I am haunted in a shimmery purple helpful way by the ancestors. And New Mexico which opens my heart is the swinging door to this, isn't it? And the aspen trees are so like the birch which helped give my Jewish family and my Norwegian family their forests."

Ánnah Sobelman was born in Los Angeles and has since lived in New York City, Northern California, and the Sangre de Cristo Mountains of Taos, NM, where she makes her home. She is a graduate of the University of Southern California, Pepperdine Law School, New York University School of Law, the University of Iowa's Writer's Workshop and in 1992–1993 attended the N.Y.U Creative Writing program. A former editor and publisher of *The Taos Review*, Ms. Sobelman is the Richard Hugo visiting poet at the University of Montana MFA program through the spring semester 1998 and teaches poetry out of her living room when she is in Taos.

Her poems have appeared in such periodicals as *The Antioch Review*, *The Boston Review*, *The Denver Quarterly*, *Indiana Review* and others. Ánnah Sobelman is the author of *The Tulip Sacrament* (Wesleyan University Press), her first collection of poetry.

"My Odessa" and "Cooking Hamantaschen" first appeared in *The Tulip Sacrament*. Reprinted by permission of the author.

RICHARD L. STEVENS

Richard L. Stevens (March 18, 1945–April 18, 1997) moved to Santa Fe from New York in 1983. He kept journals, wrote scripts, read widely, and had a rich sense of humor. In 1987 he had surgery for Renal Cell Carcinoma. He faced cancer with great inner resources, teaching others lessons he never imagined. "Schlomo's Heaven" is from *The Schlomo Papers* a series of twenty pieces that Rick and Joan Logghe wrote in collaboration during the last year of his life when he was blind due to complications from surgery. Schlomo developed into a Jewish counterpart to the Sufi character Nasrudin, a holy man/fool.

MARCIA WOLFF

"Recently, I earned my master's degree in counseling from Southwestern College. I am now in private practice as well as working as a counselor with offenders and victims of domestic violence at the District Attorney's Office. Previously, for 15 years, I was a registered psychiatric nurse.

"My writing is informed by my Jewish sensibility in that it comes out of my own experience. My own personal ethics and morals are woven through my poetry. I offer my honest experience and my ideas based on the values taught me through Judaism. The central organizing principle of my life has been Hillel's statement: 'If I am not for myself, who am I? If I am only for myself, what am I? And if not now, when?'

"New Mexico has influenced my ideas in that my moving here came out of a desire to return more to myself, to my earthy heritage, and to cycles."

INDEX

A

Agosín, Marjorie 125, 126, 155

B

Becker, Robin 54, 130, 155

E

Enson, Beth 131, 156

F

Finstein, Max 30, 31, 156
Fishman, Yehudis 35, 62, 76, 77, 80, 156
Frumkin, Gene 26, 28, 86, 157

G

Gersh, Bill 41, 107, 108, 158
Gintzler, A S. 149, 158
Goldberg, Jenny 37, 158
Goldberg, Natalie 20, 21, 39, 42, 116, 159
Gottlieb, Rabbi Lynn 84, 159

H

Hill, Judyth 97, 99, 100, 110, 117, 118, 120, 160
Hotch, Phyllis 63, 64, 113, 160

L

Lamden, Shuli 34, 73, 74, 114, 161,
Logghe, Joan 48, 52, 65, 79, 87, 92, 109, 123, 151, 161
Luz, Consuelo 82, 129, 152, 162

M

Meyers, Matt 33, 101, 163,
Moldaw, Carol 58, 83, 102, 164,
Mondragón, Elmo 140, 164

About the Cover Artist

Diana Bryer's imagery is based on the celebration of life and our relationship to each other, the animal kingdom, the changing seasons, and our Mother Earth. Each painting is a prayer for peace, for the environment, and for balance within the heart of male and female. Diana has lived with her family on a small farm in northern New Mexico since 1977. Her original paintings are in many public and private collections.

About the Press

Sherman Asher Publishing, an independent press established in 1994, is dedicated to changing the world one book at a time. We are committed to the power of truth and the craft of language expressed by publishing fine poetry, memoir, books on writing, and other books we love. You can play a role. Bring the gift of poetry into your life and the lives of others. Attend readings, teach classes, work for literacy, support your local bookstore, and buy poetry.